ENGLISH SPELLING

Edward Carney

KT-377-436

London and New York

First published 1997
by Routledge
11 New Fetter Lane, London EC4P 4EE

Simultaneously published in the USA and Canada
by Routledge
29 West 35th Street, New York, NY 10001

© 1997 Edward Carney

Typset in Times Ten and Univers by
Florencetype Limited, Stoodleigh, Devon

Printed and bound in Great Britain by
Redwood Books, Trowbridge, Wiltshire

All right reserved. No part of this book may be reprinted or reproduced or
utilized in any form or by any electronic, mechanical, or other means, now
known or hereafter invented, including photocopying and recording, or in
any information storage or retrieval system, without permission in writing
from the publishers.

British Library Cataloguing in Publication Data
A catalogue record for this book is available from the British Library.

Library of Congress Cataloguing in Publication Data
Carney, Edward.
  English Spelling / Edward Carney.
  – (Language workbooks)
  1. English Language–Orthography and spelling. I. Title.
  II. Series
  PE1143.C368 1997
  428.1–dc21   96-47573
             CIP

ISBN 0–415–16109–6 (pbk)

UNIVERSITY COLLEGE
WINCHESTER
428
372.63
CAR
02941953

CONTENTS

USING THIS BOOK

This is a workbook on present-day English spelling, but it is not just a collection of helpful hints for 'bad spellers'. Nor could a book of this size possibly be a 'complete' account of present spelling conventions. However, it tries to show the underlying regularities in English spelling and how English has coped over the centuries with the conventions introduced by borrowed words. Culture-carrying words have flooded in from French and Latin. Scientific terms have been concocted from Latin and Greek elements. History underlies the difference of spelling between *apple* and *chapel*, but we are chiefly concerned with how the ordinary person can cope with such differences today.

In a workbook such as this, you are encouraged to tackle a number of exercises on each topic, extracting for yourself patterns of spelling from data provided. Answers to exercises are given at the end of the book. Obviously, you will gain most by doing the exercises before you look up the explanation.

Since our concern is with how we write what is said and read what is written, a little elementary phonetics is provided at the start. This has been kept to a minimum. Phoneme symbols are explained with learning exercises in **Unit 2** 'Finding phonemes'. This unit also introduces the idea that spelling regularities (and problems) may be related to a speaker's accent: the spoken form of their particular dialect. Salient features of both American and British spelling are described where they differ: AmE refers to American usage and BrE to British.

At the outset, be sure to familiarise yourself with the basic linguistic terms explained on pp. 3–4, such as 'phoneme', 'consonant', 'vowel', 'diphthong', 'digraph'. It is all too easy to confuse sounds and letters.

At the end of the book there are some suggestions for further reading and a note on reference works, including *LPD* and *OED*.

ACKNOWLEDGEMENTS

I am grateful to Dick Hudson, as Editor of this Workbook series, for many suggestions and much encouragement. I am also indebted to Chris Upward for his detailed comments on the spelling reform section and to the Simplified Spelling Society for the use of their material.

SPEAKING AND WRITING

1

All human societies have language. Most societies in the modern world have worked out, or have borrowed, a system for writing down their language. They have become literate.

Writing seems to have evolved out of picture-painting some 8,000 years ago. At first, writing was used in magic rituals, astronomy and accounting. The ability to write down a message with conventional symbols added vast new power to human language even though writing is a slow and clumsy process compared with speech. To receive a spoken message you have to be within hearing distance, or the message has to pass, as rumours still do, along a chain of speakers and listeners. To store a spoken message, you need an accurate memory. At least this was so before the quite recent invention of modern sound-recording. But with the development of writing, accurate and permanent records could be kept for long periods of time. Written messages could be sent anywhere. Literature, history and law were no longer a matter of uncertain oral tradition.

We take it for granted nowadays that everyone ought to be able to read and write, but in former times the vast majority of the population was illiterate. Reading and writing were only for the wealthy and the professional classes. In the nineteenth century, with growing industrialisation and the rise in industrial societies of a middle class with an appetite for self-help, literacy became more widespread. Now literacy is regarded world-wide as a basic human right, since it is the essential key to an education for the modern world.

EXERCISES ✎

1.1 If you are reading this text, you are obviously a literate person. In a modern 'developed' society, you will assume that the people you come across in daily life are equally literate. But some, through no fault of their own, never learn to read and write. Try to imagine the difficulties of an illiterate person in such basic activities as shopping and travelling in our modern world.

On the other hand, think of the pictorial signs used in public places that do not depend on literacy or on any particular language, such as road signs and hazard warnings. Be careful to explore the cultural context and underlying assumptions. The head of a deer shown on a road sign is not an invitation to hunt. And what about those symbols on toilet doors?

Logo

1.2 In the Middle Ages each knight carried the heraldic device of his family on his shield to identify him in battle. Inns and public houses had similar traditional picture signs, such as 'The Red Lion'. Many present-day organisations have taken up this idea and have designed a modern LOGO to show their name as a single graphic sign. These logos often include the name of the organisation, or its initials, printed in a special format, or a stylised drawing of what they make and sell. Look for some logos in advertising and letter headings. What do they aim to tell you about the organisation?

ALPHABETIC WRITING

Some writing systems retain a pictorial element. The complex characters of Chinese and the hieroglyphs of ancient Egypt developed from pictorial beginnings. English, however, has an alphabetic writing system that maps letters on to speech-sounds and speech-sounds on to letters.

Alphabetic writing came about as a later development of writing systems. About 3,000 years ago, the Greeks seized on an idea that was beginning to emerge in the writing systems of their Semitic neighbours. You can represent a string of speech-sounds (strictly speaking 'phonemes') by a string of written letters, using one symbol for each phoneme and one phoneme for each symbol. The ancient Greeks developed a complete alphabet of letters for both the vowels and the consonants of Greek. The Semites had only developed symbols for consonants. Our word 'alphabet' is made up from the names of the first two letters in the list of Greek letters: the vowel letter 'alpha' <α> and the consonant letter 'beta' <β>. It is hard for us today to realise what an ingenious technological invention the alphabetic principle is. We take it for granted, like the use of the wheel.

English did not borrow its alphabet direct from the Greeks, but from the Romans, who had been quick to develop their own version. Over the centuries English spelling conventions have been strongly influenced by French. Like all borrowed garments, the roman alphabet is not a perfect fit for English. There are holes and patches, but it serves its purpose better than it is usually given credit for.

In describing the alphabetic principle, we used the term PHONEME without explanation. A phoneme is what native speakers of a language would naturally regard as a functional 'speech-sound'. Why then do we need the term phoneme, if that is all it means? Why not use 'sound' instead?

The reason is that no phoneme is a single unvarying sound. Phonemes vary somewhat from context to context and from speaker to speaker. For most English-speakers the English /l/ phoneme usually sounds different in *leap* and *peel*. The vowel in *grief* is often shorter than the 'same' vowel phoneme in *grieve*. If you say *pine* slowly you can hear a little puff of air as your lips open. After /s/ in *spine* there is little or none. Detailed description of such sound differences is the business of phonetics.

For describing how phonemes are spelt we do not need to go into such phonetic detail. However, we do have to learn a few phoneme symbols. You would no doubt become familiar with English phoneme symbols as you gradually read through the book, but it saves time in the long run to make a real effort now to learn them.

At the same time, take good notice of the kinds of bracket used in describing spelling. Letters are quoted in angled brackets < > and phonemes in slant lines / /. So we can say that the phoneme /k/ is spelt as the letters <k> in *kit*, <c> in *cat* and <ch> in *chemist*. Also the letter <c> corresponds to the phonemes /k/ in *cat*, and /s/ in *face*. Such CORRESPONDENCES can be set out in a little formula using '≡' to mean 'corresponds to'. So at the beginning of *cat* there is the correspondence <c> ≡ /k/ or, looked at the other way round, /k/ ≡ <c>.

<C> means any consonant letter and <V> any vowel letter. <C>-doubling, refers to 'consonant-letter doubling' such as the <mm> of *comma*.

1.3 Here is a list of thirty-five words. Sort them into groups according to the number of phonemes (vowels and consonants) which they have. Remember that a phoneme may be spelt by more than one letter and that some letters may be more or less redundant.

ache	ape	bath	bathe	blue	bring	buy
choice	choose	cough	debt	dough	ease	eggs
eight	half	inn	one	ought	patch	plough
right	shred	since	stray	tax	think	thread
through	twine	two	who	wrench	write	youth

This is an opportunity to check your understanding of some basic terms.

A MORPHEME is a minimal unit in the grammar of words. The word *reason* is a single morpheme, while <un+reason+able+ness>

Free morpheme
Bound morpheme

Vowel
Consonant
Vowel letter
Consonant letter

Diphthong
Digraph

consists of four. Here the letters <son> clearly do not represent such a unit: *reason* is minimal. Morphemes that can stand on their own as words are FREE; those which only occur in complex words, as do {un} or {ness}, are BOUND. Morphemes may sound rather different in different contexts. A good example is the verbal ending {-ed}. Its pronunciation varies in *wished*, *begged* and *wanted*. Morphemes are quoted in curly 'braces' as in {ness}.

In this book, and in linguistics generally, VOWEL and CONSONANT are used in a purely phonetic sense and refer to phonemes. If you want to refer to writing and spelling, then you have to say VOWEL LETTER for any letter from the set <a, e, i, o, u, y> and CONSONANT LETTER for any letter from the set <b, c, d, f, g, h, j, k, l, m, n, p, q, r, s, t, v, w, x, y, z>. Awkwardly, the letter <y> belongs to both sets.

So, when the text refers specifically to letters it says so. The word *box* ends in a consonant letter <x> which represents two consonants /ks/. A statement such as: 'the first vowel is followed by a single consonant' would apply to both *lemon* and *common*. There is a double consonant letter in *common*, but not a double consonant. You can hear a double consonant in a careful pronunciation of *wholly*, *misstate* compared with *holy*, *mistake*.

A surprising number of writers on literacy cause misunderstandings by using 'vowel' and 'consonant' for both letters and phonemes. You must watch out for such confusions. There is also widespread misuse of DIPHTHONG and DIGRAPH. The term 'diphthong', like 'vowel' and 'consonant', is purely phonetic and has nothing to do with writing. It refers to a gliding vowel sound within a single syllable, as distinct from a relatively 'pure' steady vowel. The words *by*, *mouse*, *fine*, *choice* all contain diphthongs. The words *chaos*, *react*, *poet* each have two vowels forming two syllables, so the <-ao->, <-ea-> and <-oe-> in these words are not spellings of diphthongs. Words such as *blood*, *broad*, *cause*, *good*, *head*, *laurel*, *lawn* may have a vowel spelling with two letters, but they do not contain diphthongs. They are said with a pure vowel and spelt with a vowel digraph. A digraph is a unit of writing, not of speech. It is a string of two letters. In *head* the digraph <ea> represents the vowel /e/.

You may find one or two real differences due to a speaker's accent in counting the phonemes in the words in Exercise 1.3. Some conservative speakers in the north of England may have kept an original final /g/ in *bring* as /brɪŋg/, giving it five phonemes. Such speakers will say *finger* and *bringer* as rhymes, each having a /g/. For the vast majority of speakers, *bring* is pronounced as only four phonemes without a final /g/ as /brɪŋ/. In this final position after /ŋ/, /g/ has usually been lost so that *bring* ends in the nasal phoneme /ŋ/. So the majority of speakers do not rhyme *finger* /fɪŋgə(r)/ and *bringer* /brɪŋ+ə(r)/, or *anger* and *banger*. Take care not to reinstate a lost /g/ in an over-deliberate pronunciation when counting phonemes.

SUMMARY

- English has an alphabetic writing system.
- Differences of accent between speakers can complicate the description of spelling conventions.
- The terms 'vowel', 'consonant' and 'diphthong' properly refer to sounds, not letters.

2 FINDING PHONEMES

> The job of a phoneme is to be phonetically distinct from all the other phonemes in a speaker's accent.

You can work out the phonemes of a particular language or dialect by making a series of minimal changes that can create fresh word forms. The series *pad, bad, dad, gad, mad, fad, sad, had, lad*, gives you at least nine of the usual twenty-four English consonant phonemes. You could find another five in *tail, nail, veil, rail, wail*. The pair /s/ and /z/ may sound alike, but *sip* and *zip* show you that they are distinct phonemes in English, adding /z/ to the list. Only 'minimal' changes are relevant here. You do not have a single new phoneme with *glad*, but a cluster of /g/ and /l/. You could try other contexts to find the remaining nine phonemes, such as the middle or end of a word.

Consonant phoneme symbols are easier to learn and cope with than vowel symbols. This is partly because vowels vary more from speaker to speaker. Most English-speakers have twenty-four consonant phonemes. For the fifteen phonemes we have just uncovered, the symbol is what you might expect: /p, b, t, d, g, m, n, f, v, s, z, h, l, r, w/. But be careful not to be misled by the spelling. The <s> in *easy* represents /z/, the <u> in *quick* represents /w/ and the <f> in *of* represents /v/.

The other nine consonant phonemes require a little comment:

> /k/ occurs in *key, catch, chemist, back, acclaim, quay, quite, Iraq* and as part of the /ks/ in *axe*.
> /ŋ/ occurs in *sing, drink*, and possibly *incline*.
> /θ/ occurs in *thin, both, ether*.
> /ð/ occurs in *this, bother, either*.
> /ʃ/ occurs in *show, chauffeur, fascist*.

/ʒ/ occurs in *leisure, occasion, equation.*
/tʃ/ occurs in **cheap**, **watch**.
/dʒ/ occurs in **jet**, **badge**.
/j/ occurs in **yet**, **yellow**, and as part of /juː/ in *cute*, **beauty**.

Scottish speakers have a further consonant phoneme /x/ in *loch* and possibly **technical** and in Scottish names and dialect words, such as *Auchtermuchty, pibroch* ('a lament'). This phonetic symbol [x] has nothing to do with the letter <x> of *box*. The sound /x/ is a 'fricative', one with rough audible friction, which is made with a narrow gap between the humped-up tongue and the soft palate. Scottish speakers, along with most Irish and AmE speakers, have a similar fricative phoneme /ʍ/. It is made with rounded lips and the back of the tongue raised in **which**, **what**, etc., rather like a strong whispered /w/. Alternatively this /ʍ/ can be treated as a cluster of the two phonemes /hw/.

Note that /ʒ/ is different from /z/; /ð/ is written as a cursive-looking 'd' crossed at the top; /tʃ/ is a joined-up 't' and 'ʃ'; /dʒ/ is a joined-up 'd' and 'ʒ'.

You might like to see the special symbols in a larger size:

/ŋ, θ, ð, ʃ, ʒ, tʃ, dʒ, ʍ/

EXERCISES ✎

2.1 The following grid shows twenty-four consonant phonemes in a number of different contexts. Where there is '???' in one of the slots, provide the missing word.

		(a)	(b)	(c)	(d)	(e)	(f)	(g)	(h)
1	/p/	pet	pail	–	pie	???	reap	–	???
2	/b/	bet	???	dub	buy	–	–	–	–
3	/t/	–	???	–	tie	letter	–	butt	–
4	/d/	???	dale	dud	???	–	reed	???	lead
5	/k/	–	kale	???	chi	–	???	buck	???
6	/g/	get	gale	dug	???	–	–	bug	???
7	/tʃ/	–	–	Dutch	–	lecher	???	–	leech
8	/dʒ/	jet	???	–	–	???	–	???	liege
9	/m/	???	mail	???	my	–	???	bum	–
10	/n/	net	nail	???	???	–	–	bun	???
11	/ŋ/	–	–	dung	–	–	–	???	–
12	/f/	–	???	duff	fie	–	reef	buff	leaf
13	/v/	vet	???	???	vie	–	reeve	–	???
14	/θ/	–	–	doth	thigh	–	???	–	Leith
15	/ð/	–	–	–	thy	leather	???	–	–
16	/s/	set	sail	–	???	lesser	–	bus	lease
17	/z/	–	–	does	–	–	–	???	lees
18	/ʃ/	–	shale	–	???	–	–	–	leash
19	/ʒ/	–	–	–	–	leisure	–	–	–
20	/h/	–	hail	–	???	–	–	–	–

21	/l/	let	–	???	lie	–	reel	–	–
22	/r/	–	???	–	rye	–	–	–	–
23	/w/	wet	wail	–	???	–	–	–	–
24	/j/	???	Yale	–	–	–	–	–	–

You can work out what the context is by looking at the words already given in a column. All the words down the (a) column must rhyme with /-et/: *pet*, *bet*, *get*, etc. and the words across row 4 are examples of /d/, so the missing word in (4a) is *debt*. Similarly, the missing word at the end of the first row (1h) is *leap*.

It is difficult to find a range of phoneme contrasts for the less common phonemes, such as /ʒ/ in *leisure* . For instance, /h/, /w/ and /j/ will only provide contrasts in initial position in a syllable and so will /r/ in some BrE accents. The reverse is true for /ŋ/, which will only show contrasts finally in a syllable after a short vowel, as in *bang*, *bag*, etc. The phoneme /ŋ/ does not normally occur after a long vowel. Many accents no longer have a phoneme /h/, though this may be masked by children being taught to read at school and having to distinguish *heart* and *art*, *high* and *eye*, etc.

Short vowel

2.2   The following grid shows seven SHORT VOWEL phonemes in a number of different contexts. Where there is '???' in one of the slots, provide the missing word.

		(a)	(b)	(c)	(d)	(e)	(f)	(g)
1	/ɪ/	???	hit	–	fill	lick	???	kid
2	/e/	pen	–	stead	???	–	ken	–
3	/æ/	???	hat	–	–	lack	???	cad
4	/ʊ/	–	–	???	full	look	–	could
5	/ʌ/	pun	???	stud	–	???	–	cud
6	/ɒ/	–	hot	–	–	lock	???	cod
7	/ə/	(only found in unstressed syllables; see below)						

You can see that /ɪ/ is an undotted 'i'; /æ/ is a cursive letter, joining up 'a' and 'e'; /ʊ/ is a curly-topped 'u' without a hook; /ʌ/ is a letter 'v' upside down; /ɒ/ is a cursive 'a' upside down; /ə/ is an upside-down 'e'.

You might like to see these phoneme symbols in a larger size:

/ɪ, e, æ, ʊ, ʌ, ɒ, ə/

The vowel phonemes of English often differ significantly from speaker to speaker. Check whether your accent has all seven short vowels. The vowel /ʌ/ developed out of /ʊ/ some centuries ago, but /ʌ/ did not reach the conservative north of England, where pairs such as *stud* and *stood*, *putt* and *put* both have /ʊ/. The same northern speakers probably have the long vowel of *spook* in *look*, *took*, etc. rather than /ʊ/. The vowel /ɒ/ has lost its lip-rounding in AmE generally, so that *bomb* and *balm* sound the same. For AmE use, simply turn the phonetic symbol the right way up to join /ɑː/.

Whereas the other short vowels can occur in both stressed and unstressed syllables (as with /æ/ in *antics* /'æntɪks/, *antiques* /æn'tiːks), the seventh short vowel /ə/ only occurs in unstressed syllables: *asparagus* /ə'spærəgəs/, *caravan* /'kærəvæn/ (the vertical mark shows that /'spæ/ and /'kæ/ are stressed syllables). A syllable with STRESS is said with slightly more force than the unstressed syllables in a word. You can see the vowel reduction in unstressed syllables by comparing *arithmetic* as a noun /ə'rɪθmətɪk/ and as an adjective /ærɪθ'metɪk/.

Stress

2.3 The grid below shows six LONG VOWEL phonemes in a number of different contexts. Where there is '???' in one of the slots, provide the missing word.

Long vowel

		(a)	(b)	(c)	(d)	(e)	(f)	(g)
8	/iː/	bee	???	steed	???	???	keen	–
9	/eɪ/	???	Kay	???	???	lake	???	–
10	/aɪ/	???	chi	–	file	???	kine	guide
11	/ɔɪ/	boy	???	–	foil	–	???	–
12	/uː/	boo	coo	–	???	–	–	–
13	/oʊ/	bow	–	stowed	foal	–	???	goad
14	/aʊ/	bough	cow	–	???	–	–	–

The vowel marker [ː] indicates a long pure vowel; 'pure' means 'not gliding' in quality. The other vowels written with two symbols are DIPHTHONGS: three of them glide towards [ɪ] and two towards [ʊ]. The diphthong /oʊ/ has lost most of its lip-rounding in southern England and is often written with the symbol /əʊ/.

Diphthongs

You may have noticed a difference in the general shape of the words used so far. The long vowels may or may not have a final consonant phoneme after them: *toy – toil, brow – brown, sea – seat, fee – feel*. The short vowels cannot occur at the end of such words. You can have *lid, bet, cap, dove, push*, but you cannot have words such as */lɪ/, */be/, */kæ/, */dʌ/, */pʊ/. Because of this, some writers prefer to call the long vowels 'FREE' and the short vowels 'CHECKED', by the need for a final consonant. (Note that we mark theoretical examples with an asterisk '*'. You will find asterisks also used to indicate spelling mistakes: *<horrorscope>.)

Free vowel Checked vowel

2.4 To deal with the remaining vowel phonemes of different English-speakers we need to know, curiously enough, how much they use the consonant phoneme /r/. Test yourself by saying the following sentence smoothly and fairly quickly.

Do remember to answer his very absurd letter.

Everybody will say /r/ at the beginning of *remember*. Where else in this utterance would you yourself actually say a phoneme /r/? Be sure to consider this carefully before reading on and do not be hijacked by the spelling.

Discussion

You can work out from the way you said this sentence which of two general types of accent is yours. It may be that you say a phoneme /r/ for every instance here of written <r>: <do remember to answer his very absurd letter>. In this case your accent is RHOTIC (or '/r/-ful'), as is most AmE, Scottish or Irish English. Rhotic accents are also found in south-west England and in parts of Lancashire. For such speakers an original /r/ is kept in all contexts indicated by an <r(r)> spelling.

Rhotic accent

Non-rhotic accent

Otherwise your accent will prove to be NON-RHOTIC (= '/r/-depleted'). As a non-rhotic speaker you may have no further /r/ at all in the example sentence other than the /r/ before a vowel in <remember> and in <very>. At your choice, you may have a so-called linking /r/ where a vowel follows immediately in the next word, as in <answer 'is>, with a loss of /h/. A non-rhotic speaker will keep an /r/ only before a following closely linked vowel, but not before a consonant or before silence or a boundary.

If you are a *rhotic* speaker you may have three further vowels plus a following /r/ in words such as these:

15 /ɔː+r/ in *door, store, before, explore, court, divorced, torn, board.*

16 /ɑː+r/ in *bar, cigar, star, starred, sharp, guard, lark, heart, market.*

17 /ɜː+r/ in *fur, defer, blur, whirr, skirt, search, nervous, burden.*

Some Scottish speakers have a distinct spelling advantage if, instead of a common /ɜː/, they differentiate the vowels of *herd, third, curd* as short vowels /e/, /ɪ/, /ʌ/ plus /r/.

A *non-rhotic* speaker would only have a phoneme /r/ actually present before a vowel, as in *storing, store it, far away,* but not before a consonant, as in *stored, store them, doorway, nervous.*

The long vowels /ɔː/ and /ɑː/ will also occur in other contexts without /r/:

15 /ɔː/ in *saw, draw, caught, sought, taunt, laundry, chalk, small.*

16 /ɑː/ in *bra, spa, palm, locale, palaver, soprano, finale,* and in southern England *past, answer, craft, dance, glass, bath* (where in northern England and in AmE there is short /æ/).

Non-rhotic accents may have diphthongs gliding to /ə/ where an /r/ has been lost:

18 /ɪə/ in *gear, steer, sincere, interfere, dreary,* where a rhotic accent would have /iːr/. The diphthong /ɪə/ also comes about without /r/ as a merger of two vowels in: *idea, meteor, jovial, media, museum.*

19 /eə/ in *bare, fair, swear, where, declare, beware, welfare, stared, prayer, cairn,* where a rhotic accent would have /eɪː+r/.

20 /(j)ʊə/ in *boor, cure, gourd, poor, sure, tour*. For many non-rhotic speakers this glide has merged with /ɔː/, so that *Shaw, shore, sure* sound the same.

Transcriptions in this book show all original /r/ phonemes as found in rhotic accents. An /r/ that is or may be lost in non-rhotic accents is shown in parentheses: /ən əb'sɜː(r)d 'letə(r)/. Sometimes an 'intrusive' /r/ is inserted by present-day speakers simply to keep two vowels apart in running speech: *That's the news from Sarah and me* as /'seərər əm 'miː/. This may happen even within a word, with *drawing* as /'drɔːrɪŋ/ or *Kafkaesque* as /kæfkə'resk/, as if the name were *<Kafker>*, not *Kafka*. Intrusive /r/ is not represented in normal spelling.

▬▬▬▬▬▬▬▬▬▬▬▬▬

This hasty review of English phonemes and the way they vary across different speakers leaves many questions unanswered, but it should be enough to allow us to examine the English writing system even-handedly for speakers with different accents. Finer phonetic detail than this in the accents of different speakers is mostly not relevant to mapping phonemes on to spellings.

If in doubt about the phonemic make-up of a word, consult *LPD* (see p. 94).

▬▬▬▬▬▬▬▬▬▬▬▬▬ **EXERCISES** ✎

2.5 Here are a few words in a phonemic transcription that you should now be able to read:

/kwɪk/   /'sɜː(r)vɪs/   /juːθ/   /ʧeə(r)z/   /ʤɔɪn/   /hɑː(r)ʃ/
/θɔːt/   /'treʒə(r)/   /aɪ'dɪə/   /'hʌŋgə(r)/   /ðouz/   /ʃæŋk/

──────────────

2.6 In writing English we sometimes use graphic symbols that are not made up of ordinary letters. These include punctuation marks, such as <!> and <?>. We also use signs in written texts such as <&>, <%>, <♥>. These have the meaning of 'and', 'per cent', 'heart', but do not contain information about how they are pronounced in English. The symbol <&> was borrowed from Latin manuscripts as a scribbled form of <et>, the Latin word for *and*. What looks like a letter <x> in biology actually means 'crossed with', indicating a hybrid. You should be able to think of a dozen more such graphic signs with ease.

──────────────

2.7 Pronunciation is partly ignored in ABBREVIATIONS such as   **Abbreviation**
<Mr>. If you want to read <Mr> aloud, you have to unpack it as /'mɪstə(r)/. Indeed, to understand properly what an abbreviation may refer to, you have to know what the particular topic is. A simple abbreviation <c.> may refer to *calorie, candle, cent, centime, century,*

conservative, *contralto*, and indeed other terms. Find further examples of abbreviations that vary in meaning, depending on what the topic is. Most large dictionaries have lists of common abbreviations.

SUMMARY

- Differences of accent between speakers, particularly in the case of vowels, can complicate the description of spelling conventions and hence the task of learning to read and write.
- The most important difference in accents is that between rhotic and non-rhotic.

LONG AND SHORT VOWEL PAIRS

3

> Single vowel letters may represent either a short or a long vowel phoneme, as in *bit* and *bite*, usually with some marker to show which is meant, like that final <-e>. Why are such vowel pairs, spelt with the same letter, so very different phonetically? In learning to read you have been told they were 'the same' apart from their length difference, so it is difficult to realise that, as sounds, they are phonetically quite different. Here we require a little history.

Our borrowed roman alphabet was designed for the simple five-vowel system of Latin, using the letters <a>, <e>, <i>, <o> and <u>. The letter <u> was originally written as <v> by the Romans, but this sharply angled <v> shape is now used separately from <u> as a consonant letter. The misguided notion that 'there are *five vowels in English' simply means that we have five roman *letters* at our disposal for making up vowel spellings, along with <y> as a sixth.

SPELLING WITH SINGLE VOWEL LETTERS

English has round about twenty vowel phonemes, depending on the speaker's accent, so it is not surprising that the vowel letters of the roman alphabet have had to be augmented by complex spellings using two or more letters such as <oo>, <oi>, <ou>, <ow>, <ai>, <ea>, <eau>. Over the centuries, as the pronunciation of words has changed, the English writing system has acquired even more complex vowel spellings such as the <aigh>, <eigh>, <igh>, <ough> of *straight*, *weight*, *fight* and *through*. The <gh> spelling in these words is the footprint of a lost consonant.

In English spelling the simple vowel letters <a>, <e>, <i>, <o> and <u> have each to cater for a pair of vowel phonemes, one short and one long. The long values are:

    <a> ≡ /eɪ/ *caper*   <e> ≡ /iː/ *meter*   <i> ≡ /aɪ/ *liner*
    <o> ≡ /oʊ/ *sofa*   <u> ≡ /(j)uː/ *putrid, lucid*

Note that these long vowel values represent the 'names' of the letters: *the letter 'a'* is said as /ðə ˈletə(r) ˈeɪ/.

Before /r/ the long vowel values are slightly different, since there is usually an [ə] glide to the /r/:

    <a> ≡ /eə/ *carer*   <e> ≡ /ɪə/ *era*   <i> ≡ /aɪə/ *wiry*
    <o> ≡ /ɔː/ *oral*   <u> /(j)ʊə/ *cure, boor*

The usual short values of the simple vowel letters are:

    <a> ≡ /æ/ *mat*   <e> ≡ /e/ *met*   <i> ≡ /ɪ/ *bit*
    <o> ≡ /ɒ/ *pot* (but in AmE /ɑː/)   <u> ≡ /ʌ/ *cut*

The present-day long and short values of <a>, <e>, <i>, <o> and <u> spellings are surprisingly different as sounds. Why is it that <i> ≡ /aɪ/, a diphthong gliding from a tongue position low in the mouth, is paired up with a short <i> ≡ /ɪ/, which has a high tongue position? They do not seem very similar as sounds. Why are the other vowel pairings equally out of kilter?

Over the last four or five centuries, the long vowels of English, as they were at about 1300, have gradually changed their phonetic quality, while the short vowels have remained relatively unchanged. As a consequence of these changes, known as the Great Vowel Shift, there is now a wide phonetic difference between pairs of vowels which originally had the same quality and which then only differed in being long and short. The writing system for the most part retains that spelling in spite of the phonetic change. This is one of the principal ways in which written English preserves a constant spelling of the same morpheme.

The gradual change of the long vowels is plotted in Table 3.1. You can best see the effects of the Great Vowel Shift in different variants of the same element of word structure (a 'morpheme'). Take the /aɪ/–/ɪ/ variation of *define* – *definitive, divine* – *divinity, decide* – *decision*. The base forms *define, divine, decide,* had a long high vowel /iː/ in Middle English (*c.* 1300). When added Latinate suffixes such as <-itive>, <-ity> or <-ion> pushed this stem vowel to the third syllable from the end of the word, the vowel was usually shortened

Table 3.1 The effect on long vowels of the Great Vowel Shift

At 1300 →	By 1400 →	By 1500 →	By 1600 →	By 1700 →	Now	Key-word
iː	ɪi	ʌi	→	→	/aɪ/	rise
uː	ʊu	ʌu	→	→	/aʊ/	mouth
eː	→	iː	→	→	/iː/	meet
oː	→	uː	→	→	/uː/	goose
ɛː	→	→	eː	→	/iː/	meat
ɔː	→	→	oː	→	/oʊ/	stone
aː	→	æː	ɛː	eː	/eɪ/	name

to /ɪ/ by a general sound change called 'third-syllable shortening'. So the morpheme originally had a matching pair of long and short vowels with the same phonetic quality /iː/ and /ɪ/. Then over the years the long vowel gradually changed into the present-day diphthong /aɪ/. The same mismatch also occurred in other contexts, such as before the ending <-ic> or <-ical>, as in *mime – mimic*. Similar phonetic distancing affected the other long/short vowel pairs.

EXERCISE ✎

Allomorph

3.1 Here is a range of words with matching long and short vowels in different forms (ALLOMORPHS, p. 4) of the same morpheme. Suggest a suitable example for the missing words indicated by '???'.

- <a> spelling for /eɪ/–/æ/ (including /eə(r)/–/ær/)

chaste – chastity	??? – gratitude	hilarious – ???
??? – humanity	mania – ???	??? – opacity
state – ???	pale – ???	??? – sanity
shade – ???	tenacious – ???	??? – valley

  The long /eɪ/ has an <ai> spelling in:

grain – granary	Spain – ???	vain – ???

- <e> spelling for /iː/–/e/ (including /ɪə(r)/–/er/)

austere – ???	??? – credulous	female – ???
helix – ???	hero – ???	??? – legislate
obscene – ???	severe – ???	supreme – ???

  The long /iː/ has an <ea> or <ee> spelling in some native words:

bereave – ???	clean – ???	heal – ???
??? – heather	seat – ???	sheep – ???

- <i> and <y> spelling for /aɪ/–/ɪ/ (including /aɪə(r)/–/ɪr/)

??? – biblical	??? – criminal	??? – definitive
five – ???	line – ???	??? – lyric
mime – ???	??? – mineral	reconcile – ???
??? – residual	satire – ???	??? – typical

- <o> spelling for /oʊ/ – /ɒ/ (including /ɔː(r)/ – /ɒr/)

??? – atrocity	??? – closet	coal – ???
floral – ???	holy – ???	omen – ???
provoke – ???	??? – solitude	??? – tonic

- the /aʊ/ – /ʌ/ examples differ from other pairings, since the /aʊ/ now has a digraph spelling, usually <ou>, and the matching short vowel for most speakers has changed to /ʌ/.

house – husband	renounce – ???	south – ???

Allomorph pairs highlight the present phonetic discrepancy in the simple <a>, <e>, <i>, <o> and <u> vowel spellings, but it is important to realise that all the Middle English long vowels were affected by the vowel shift in words such as *leaf*, *feed*, *green*, *peep*, *sweet*, *loud*, *down*, *town*, *doom*, *mood*, *lame*, *save*, *game*, etc.

Figure 3.1 shows the results of the vowel shift. The present-day vowels are grouped phonetically into front and back with three degrees of tongue height: high, mid and low. So the pair /iː/–/ɪ/ are in the top left corner as high and front. The original pairs of long and short vowels are connected with lines, so you can see that the /iː/–/ɪ/ of *metre* and *linear* belong to different structural pairings: /iː/ has the short counterpart /e/ and /ɪ/ has the long counterpart /aɪ/.

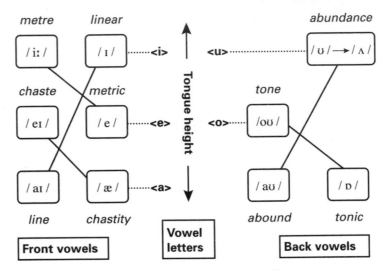

Figure 3.1 The results of the Great Vowel Shift

SUMMARY

- The pairs of vowels, long and short, that are found in variants of the same morpheme, as in *line – linear*, are phonetically dissimilar, since the original long vowels have changed phonetically over the centuries. These changes are called 'the Great Vowel Shift'.

MARKING VOWEL LENGTH

4

> Consonant-letter doubling, as in *mill*, and final <-e> as in *mile*, combine to determine the pronunciation of the single basic vowel letters <a>, <e>, <i>, <o>, <u> and <y>.

Since the single letters <a>, <e>, <i>, <o>, <u> and <y> can represent either a short vowel phoneme or a long vowel phoneme, the English writing system must be able to mark which value is intended. In a word such as *comma*, the doubled consonant letter marks the previous vowel as short /ɒ/. In *coma*, which has long /oʊ/, there is no consonant-letter doubling. Similarly we find:

latter /æ/ – later /eɪ/	vellum /e/ – velum /iː/
stripped /ɪ/ – striped /aɪ/	rudder /ʌ/ – ruder /uː/

To avoid having to write 'consonant-letter doubling' all the time, we can shorten it to '<C>-DOUBLING', remembering that it is only a doubling of letters, not of phonemes. The capital <C> here stands for any consonant and symbols in angled brackets < > refer to letters, not to sounds. The digraph spelling in *latter, vellum, stripped, comma, rudder* only stands for one single consonant phoneme, just as does the single letter of *later, velum, striped, coma, ruder*.

<C>-doubling

The vowel letter <y> is sometimes marked by <C>-doubling: *abyss, hyssop, idyll,* but rather more commonly in names: *Flynn, Lymm, Lytton, Phyllis.*

Since a previous short vowel is normally involved, we only see doubling at the beginning of a word in rare cases: the <Ll> and <Ff> of Welsh names such as *Lloyd, Llanrwst, Ffestiniog.* There are occasional foreign loans, such as *llama,* which is effectively marked as a foreign word by the doubling.

The problem is that you cannot always expect a doubled letter spelling after every short vowel. In words borrowed from Latin and

French we may well find <C>-doubling marking the vowel as short, as in *comma, horrid, callous, annual*. However, there are words of Latin and French origin, such as *comet, florid, honour*, where the short vowel is not marked. Indeed, there is both *cannon* ('gun') and *canon* ('priest'). What is clear is that for the reader, doubled consonant letters mark a previous short vowel. How the long vowel values might be marked will be discussed later.

EXERCISE ✎

4.1 This exercise will assume that you are now familiar with the symbols for consonant phonemes, of which there are twenty-four in most accents of English:

/p, b, t, d, k, g, ʧ, ʤ, m, n, ŋ, f, v, θ, ð, s, z, ʃ, ʒ, h, l, r, w, j/

Which of these phonemes may have <C>-doubling with the same letter repeated, such as the <-pp-> of *supper*, to mark a previous short vowel? Give an example word for each such phoneme.

The reason why it is convenient to use a doubled spelling to mark a short vowel is that long vowels normally do not occur before two consonant phonemes in the general run of simple words such as *belt, cost, disc, film, hamper, hand, lift, pulp, whisper*.

One important restriction is that <C>-doubling does not occur when the previous vowel in the morpheme is spelt with more than one letter, so *heading* is not spelt *<headding>. Here the <dd> would in fact be quite a useful short vowel marker because of the competing long vowel in *pleading, reading*.

EXERCISE ✎

4.2 Three other phonemes /k, ʧ, ʤ/ have spellings that are not actual repetitions of the same letter, but which seem to mark the shortness of the vowel nevertheless. Give some examples of native English words by way of explanation.

The spellings <cc> and <kk> are clearly not found in native English words.

Doubled <cc> may represent /ks/, with Latinate prefixes as in *accept, accident*, and simple /k/ in *account, accompany, occupy, succumb*. The <cc> spelling of /k/ is otherwise only found in more or less 'exotic' words:

broccoli	buccaneer	desiccate	ecclesiastic	felucca
mecca	moccasin	peccadillo	piccalilli	piccolo
staccato	streptococci	stucco	tobacco	yucca

Seen as a group, these words with <cc> are all to some extent exotic, whereas <ck> only occurs in native words. Yet *tobacco*, exotic in origin, has become commonplace enough. It is difficult to lay down criteria for what is 'exotic' in meaning. If you feel *yucca* to be an exotic plant, you will not expect a native appearance as *<yucker>. On the other hand *gecko*, which is undoubtedly an exotic animal, has <ck>.

The spelling <kk> is much less common and occurs in an occasional loan-word such as *chukker* (in polo), *trekking* (from *trek*), and exotic names, as *Akkad, Dekker, Fokker, Hokkaido, Sikkim*.

The single-letter spelling <j>, commonly associated with /ʤ/, occurs initially in words such as *jar, jaw, job, juice*, or in Latinate stems such as *inject, conjunction, rejuvenate*, so there is no possible context for a doubled *<jj>.

The remaining eight consonant phonemes are not involved with <C>-doubling for various reasons. In stressed syllables /h/, /w/ and /j/, as in *hot, wit, yet*, only occur initially and /ŋ, θ, ð, ʃ, ʒ/ do not have independent single-letter spellings to double. The system does not allow *<washshing>, *<boththter> for *washing, bother*.

EXERCISES ✎

4.3 If <C>-doubling marks a vowel as short, why do we find spellings such as the following rather than *<biggamy>, *<carravan>? What do these words have in common?

bigamy	caravan	cataract	celery	character
copula	criminal	denizen	elephant	faculty
heroine	nemesis	obscenity	ominous	perspicacity
sanity	solitude	strategy	tabulate	vilify

Discussion

These are all words in which the syllable with primary stress is the third from the end of the word. Moreover there are no prefixes or suffixes that can be detached to leave a shorter word, as there would be in *likelihood, carelessness, shrubbery*. They are minimal free forms.

For various reasons the third syllable from the end of a minimal free form is very unlikely to be marked by <C>-doubling. As we have just seen, a 'minimal free form' is a word that can stand on its own as an utterance, without separable parts. Any such forms of three or more syllables are unlikely to be words of native English origin and probably came from Latin or Greek, where doubled consonant letters are uncommon.

We have already seen that some morphemes have a long vowel spelt by single letter <a, e, i, o, u> which becomes short when it is pushed into the third syllable from the end of the word by added suffixes, such as *sane, sanity*. This is called third-syllable shortening. There is no <C>-doubling to mark this shortened vowel: the writing system keeps the spelling of the morpheme constant with a single consonant letter. This accounts for the lack of <C>-doubling in *criminal, heroine, obscenity, ominous, sanity, solitude, tabulate, vilify*.

Usually there is no <C>-doubling to mark the short first vowel in other words of three syllables which do not have obvious related forms with a long vowel. Examples are: *bigamy, caravan, cataract, celery, character, copulate, denizen, elephant, faculty, nemesis, pelican, prodigal, strategy.*

In consequence, we can narrow down the contexts in which <C>-doubling will occur in practice: a stressed short vowel is marked by <C>-doubling when it occurs in the last two syllables of a minimal free form.

A minimal free form, as we have seen, is the smallest free-standing unit of word structure. This includes words such as *back, edge, full, itch, miss, stiff, happy, hobby, otter, pillow, summer, goggle, spaghetti, armadillo.* These free forms may have prefixes and suffixes attached to them without affecting the <C>-doubling: *backwardly, stiffly, itchiness, unhappiness.*

There is no <C>-doubling, naturally enough, if a consonant is initial in a recurrent element of word structure: *product*, not *<prodduct>, since the <d> is initial in the *duct* element.

4.4 We have seen that <C>-doubling is used to mark a preceding stressed vowel as short. Sometimes a final <-e> marks the previous vowel as long. Consider the following words:

	short	*long*	*short*	*long*
1	/ɪ/ till	/aɪ/ tile	/ɪ/ tilling	/aɪ/ tiling
2	/æ/ tap	/eɪ/ tape	/æ/ tapping	/eɪ/ taping

How is vowel length marked here? Which consonant letters follow the pattern in (1) above when doubled and which follow pattern (2)?

4.5 Does the final <-e> in the following words serve any useful purpose?

adze	bathe	breathe	bronze	browse
cleanse	copse	corpse	crease	else
freeze	house	lapse	loathe	maize
parse	please	praise	tease	tense

4.6 If you add a suffix to a word ending in <-e>, when is the <-e> deleted before the suffix and when does it remain? Comment on the following examples.

agree+ing	bathe+ing	blue+ish	browse+ing	cadge+ing
canoe+ing	change+ing	elope+ment	fatigue+ing	festive+ity
fine+ly	gauge+able	glue+ing	hate+ful	hinge+ing
judge+ment	like+able	loathe+ing	love+ing	manage+ment

mate+ed	mate+ing	mile+age	mode+ish	move+ing
notice+able	pale+ish	pale+ness	plague+ing	rescue+ing
sale+able	singe+ing	tease+ing	trace+able	value+ing

SUMMARY

■ A stressed vowel may be marked as short by a following doubled consonant letter in the last two syllables of a minimal free form.

■ A final <-e> after a single consonant letter in native words will mark the previous vowel as long. This <-e> is usually dropped if a suffix beginning with a vowel is added.

■ 'Lexical <-e>' marks *lapse*, *tense*, etc. as single morphemes.

■ When final in a monosyllabic word, /z/ and /ð/ may be marked by a final <-e> even when they occur after two vowel letters, as in *please*, *wreathe*.

5 COMPLICATIONS IN LENGTH MARKING

Some groups of words prove exceptions to the rules that govern consonant-letter doubling in native English words.

EXERCISE ✎

5.1 There are unexpected doubled letters in some quite common short words. Can you see any reason for the difference in spelling between the two-letter words and the three-letter words in the following list?

add	am	as	at	awe	axe	be	bo
do	ebb	egg	eye	go	he	id	if
in	inn	is	it	lo	low	me	odd
of	on	or	ore	owe	ox	pa	pi
pie	she	ti	to	too	up	us	we

The following two-syllable words with stress on the short vowel of the first syllable do not have <C>-doubling, though this is a context where you would expect it.

adult	agate	agile	atom	baton	bigot
body	brigand	cabin	chapel	city	copy
digit	dragon	figure	flagon	fragile	frigate
image	legate	legume	leper	medal	metal
model	modern	pageant	pedal	petal	pigeon
pity	plateau	proper	rebel (n.)	ribald	riband
rigour	robin	satin	shadow	spigot	study
sugar	treble	triple	vigil	vigour	widow

Indeed, when used as a personal name there may well be doubling, as in *Boddy*, *Chapple*, *Pidgeon*.

With the hindsight of history, we can say that many of these words were borrowed into English from medieval French and Latin. Many more followed in the sixteenth century, with *petal* and *plateau* as late as the eighteenth century. The only three native words here that have come through from Old English are *body*, *shadow* and *widow*.

Over the centuries, the pronunciation of these loan-words has become more English. In *chapel*, for instance, the <ch> now represents /ʧ/, not French /ʃ/. So there is little in the present phonetic shape of these words to mark them as different from native words. Indeed, there are false spelling analogies to be made between such a loan-word and a word with native doubling:

> city – ditty   leper – pepper   medal – meddle metal – mettle
> pedal – peddle proper – copper robin – bobbin   treble – pebble

These exceptions to <C>-doubling are clearly a problem for the speller, but other distinct groups of words prove more predictable.

EXERCISES

5.2 The following words also have a stressed short vowel which is not marked as short by <C>-doubling. Why do we not have *<fridgid>, *<stattic> instead of *frigid*, *static*? What do these words have in common?

acid	arid	athletic	avid	conic
eugenic	euphoric	fetid	florid	frigid
globule	granule	intrepid	lyric	manic
mimic	module	nodule	paralytic	placid
rigid	schedule	solid	static	stolid
tepid	timid	tonic	vapid	vivid

5.3 The following words have a stressed short vowel in the syllable before the ending <-ish>. In some words the vowel is marked as short by <C>-doubling and in other words not. Is there any possible explanation? Are there any exceptions?

abolish	astonish	banish	blemish	bullish
cherish	clannish	donnish	finish	flourish
hellish	hoggish	lavish	mannish	nourish
parish	piggish	polish	priggish	punish
radish	raffish	reddish	relish	rubbish
Scottish	skittish	sluggish	snobbish	vanish

5.4 The long vowel value of a single <a, e, i, o, u, y> is fairly predictable before certain unstressed endings, but sometimes, contrary to expectations, there is a short vowel, without <C>-doubling, as in:

moral   salary   clement   lemon   valour/valor

You are asked to find a few sample words with the more common long vowel before each of these particular endings.

5.5   The following words end in an unstressed syllable with a short vowel. Normally you would not expect this unstressed vowel to be marked by <C>-doubling. However, some of these final consonants do have <C>-doubling before endings such as <-ed> or <-ing>. Sort out the following words into those which do and those which do not.

ballot	banquet	beckon	bias	bigot
bivouac	bus	carol	carpet	channel
chirrup	combat	cosset	counsel	credit
differ	duel	equal	focus	format
gallop	gossip	handicap	hiccup	kidnap
label	level	marshal	model	offer
orphan	pencil	picnic	proffer	quarrel
rocket	signal	suffer	summon	toboggan
traffic	travel	vomit	wallop	worship

The following words originate in Latin. They all begin with what was a Latin prefix. The meaning of the prefix and the stem in these examples can be guessed, even if you have little or no Latin, by comparing them with other words in which the elements recur. Note that the prefix {in-} has two different meanings 'not' and 'in(to)'.

{ab-} – *aberrant* ('from' + 'wander'); cf. *err, erratic*;
{ad-} – *adoption* ('close to' + 'choose'); cf. *option*;
{con-} – *concurrent* ('along with' + 'running'); cf. *recurrent*;
{ex-} – *excrescent* ('out of' + 'growing'); cf. *crescent moon*;
{in-} ('not') – *indignity* ('not' + 'worthy'); cf. *dignified, dignity*;
{in-} ('in(to)') – *incur* ('into' + 'run'); cf. *current*;
{inter-} – *intersection* ('between' + 'cutting'); cf. *section, sector, bisect*;
{ob-} – *obstruction* ('in the way of' + 'build'); cf. *structure*;
{per-} – *perspire* ('through' + 'breathe'); cf. *inspire, conspire*;
{sub-} – *subterranean* ('under' + 'the earth'); cf. *territory*.

These elements often recur in Latinate terms. If we know that *adjacent* means 'lying close to', the meaning of the much rarer *interjacent* or *subjacent* is clear enough. Quite often, however, the link has become obscure, as in the case of *addiction* ('habit') and *diction* ('speech'). It is all too easy to make a wrong association: the word *sect* looks as if it were related to *section* by meaning 'cut off from other people'. It is, however, from the root {sequ} meaning 'to follow', as in *sequel, consequence.*

5.6 Each of the words in the following list begins with a Latinate prefix, but the form of the prefix may differ from the basic form shown above. Is there any purely phonetic reason why the prefixes have a different appearance in these words? Note especially that where the prefix and the stem meet, the spelling may have doubled consonant letters. These are highlighted in the text.

> {ad-} *acclaim, accumulate, affect, affluent, agglomerate* ('to heap together'), *aggregate, alleviate, allocate, appreciate* ('to value at a price'), *approximate, assimilate* ('to make like to'), *attenuate, attract* ('to draw to');
>
> {con-} *collaboration, collapse, collision, commercial, commission, connect, connive, connubial, correspond, corrugated, corruption;*
>
> {ex-} *efface, effect, effeminate, efficient;*
>
> {in-} ('not') *illicit* ('not lawful'), *illiterate, immaculate* ('unblemished'), *immediate, immense* ('not measurable'), *impolite;*
>
> {in-} ('in(to)') *illuminate, immigrant, imminent, immure* ('to wall in'), *impending, import, irrigate, irruption* ('breaking in'); *irritate* seems to fit, but the Latin origin is obscure;
>
> {ob-} *occasion* ('falling at'), *occident* ('setting'), *occupy, occur, offend, opportune* ('near the harbour' = 'convenient'), *oppose, oppress;*
>
> {per-} *pellucid* ('thoroughly lucid');
>
> {sub-} *succeed, succinct, succumb, summon.*

The {sur-} of *surmise, surmount, surname, surpass, surplice,* is not from Latin {sub-} 'under' but Latin {super-} 'over'.

Discussion

In a Latinate word like *adduce,* the <-dd-> comes at a boundary between a prefix part <ad-> and a stem part <-duce>. Doubled letters occur in the same way with some modern English prefixes as in *misstate, unnatural.* Here the boundary between the prefix <mis-> and the stem <-state> is clear and the pronunciation is usually a geminate ('twinned') /-ss-/, /-nn-/.

Assimilation

The Latinate prefixes are complicated by changes in spelling to match the consonant at the beginning of the stem to which they are attached. This process is called ASSIMILATION. So the prefix <ad-> becomes <ac-> in *acquire,* <af-> in *affect,* <ap-> in *approve,* <an-> in *announce;* <ex-> becomes <ef-> in *effusive;* <in-> becomes <im-> in *immerse,* <il-> in *illegal;* <ob-> becomes <oc-> in *occlude,* <of-> in *offend.* Normally the two letters of these double spellings <-ff->, <-ll->, <-mm->, <-nn->, <-pp->, etc., correspond to a single consonant phoneme in the present-day English forms.

In some cases where the following stem represents a free form (*illegal, immodest,*) and where the prefix is clearly additive in terms of meaning, a formal pronunciation may produce a geminate ('twinned') consonant phoneme /-ll-/, /-mm-/, etc. Normally there is a single phonetic consonant in such cases, as in /ɪ'liːgl̩/ *illegal.*

Although {ad}+{tract} gives a <-tt-> in *attract*, and {ad}+{sent} gives a <-ss-> in *assent*, there is one restriction worth noting. If the Latin stem begins with an <-sC-> cluster, there is no <-ss->, but only single <-s->. So we have *ascribe, aspect, ascend, dispirited, distance, transpire*, not *<asscribe>, *<disstance>, *<transspire>, etc. This does not apply to the English prefix {mis-}, as in *misspent, misstate*, which is different in that it is a productive prefix added to free forms.

The <-CC-> letter clusters associated with these Latin prefixes resemble the doubling that marks short vowels and the vowels of the prefixes are indeed short. So, many such clusters will be covered by the ordinary doubling rules, as are nouns such as *affix* /'æfɪks/, *annexe*, etc. However, the <-CC-> found with prefixes does represent a spelling problem because in many instances the prefix vowel is unstressed and reduced to /ə/, as in the verbs *affix* /ə'fɪks/, *commute* /kə'mjuːt/, *oppose* /ə'pəʊz/, etc. The reduced vowel in the prefix may cause confusion with other reduced syllables followed by a single consonant letter. Spellers have to distinguish *allure* from *alight*, *illegal* from *elope*, *affront* from *afraid*, etc. *Aquatic* and *aquiline*, which come from Latin <aqua> 'water' and <aquila> 'eagle', are frequently mis-spelt as *<acquatic>, *<acquiline>, on the wrong model of *acquaint, acquire, acquit*, which have a prefix <ad-> modified as <ac->.

Anyone who can associate the Latin elements <ab->, <ad->, <-err->, <-brev-> with meanings 'from', 'to', 'wander' and 'short', might be able to see a reason for the difference in spelling between such pairs as <ab-> and <abb-> in *aberrant* and *abbreviate*. The strongest form of literacy involves learning the meaning of some of the Latin and Greek elements in our vocabulary. The best chance of this is with those words, such as *illegal* or *aberrant*, where the stem is an independent free form (*legal, errant*), so that prefix and stem are still separable.

5.7 Many words contain a Latin element which keeps its doubled letter in derived forms. Recognising such elements by their meaning is not always easy. The basic sense of {mitt} 'send' is apparent in *remittance* and, with its {miss} variant, in *missile*, but it is hardly recognisable by its meaning in *committee* and *permission*.

Give examples of derived words containing the following Latinate elements in which the doubled letter is outside the usual contexts for <C>-doubling in native words:

| {ann/enn} 'year' | {bell} 'war' | {fall} 'deceit' | {flamm} 'fire' |
| {horr} 'dread' | {narr} 'relate' | {terr} 'earth' | {terr} 'fear' |

5.8   Does the ending <-ion> always have a previous double <-ll->
(rather than single) in words such as *million*?

SUMMARY

- Lexical words are usually spelt with a minimum of three
  letters by exploiting <e>-marking or vowel digraphs or <C>-
  doubling where appropriate. Most function words only have
  two letters.
- Two identical consonant letters may occur in words with
  a Latinate prefix (<ad->, <com->, <e(x)->, <in->, <ob->,
  <per->, <sub->) as in *adduce, command, innate*.
- The endings <-ic>, <-id>, <-ule>, usually indicate a short
  vowel in the stem.

6

SOME CONSONANT SPELLINGS

English spelling often shows divergence from the alphabetic principle of only one spelling for each phoneme and only one phoneme for each spelling. This unit explores some of the divergence found in consonant spellings.

EXERCISES

6.1 How many different phonemes are spelt by <th> in the following words? Is there any way of knowing which word has which phoneme?

Anthony	bath	bathe	both	bother	brother
cathode	ether	frothy	lather	mammoth	method
orthodox	Thailand	Thames	that	the	then
Theodore	there	thigh	think	this	Thomas
thread	thyme	toothsome	wither	wreath	wreathe

6.2 As you might expect, <g> usually spells /g/ in words such as:

(a)
ago	anger	disgust	finger	garden	gather
glow	goat	good	great	gum	ingot

However the letter <g> frequently forms a /dʒ/ spelling, as in:

(b)
agile	allergic	apology	deluge	digit	energetic
engage	engine	fragile	frigid	gel	gem
genial	gesture	gin	ginger	giraffe	gist
gymnast	gypsum	huge	large	magic	page
pigeon	refugee	stage	stranger	vigil	wage

There are also words like the following to consider:

(c) beguile   dialogue   fatigue   guarantee   guard   guess
    guest   guide   guild   guillotine   guilty guitar
    guy   league   rogue   synagogue   vague   vogue

How is the spelling arranged to make it possible for <g> to represent both /g/ and /dʒ/? Can you think of any words that would not
fit into this arrangement?

6.3   Some letters in a word may appear to be superfluous. Are there
any such 'silent' letters' in the following words that may be dispensed
with? Or do some of these letters have a useful purpose by indicating links with related words?

two   receipt   hasten   sign
debt   doubt   bomb   dumb   lamb

6.4   How many different phonemes are spelt by <ch> in the
following groups of words?

(a) beech   beseech   birch   cheap   cheese
    child   church   reach   speech   teach
(b) achieve   approach   archer   attach   chair
    chamber   chaste   peach   rich   touch
(c) cache   creche   gauche   moustache   niche
(d) brochure   cachet   chagrin   chalet   chandelier
    charlatan chevron   chic   chivalry   echelon
    machine   nonchalant parachute   ricochet   sachet
(e) anarchy   architect   bronchitis catechism   chaos
    character chemistry   chiropodist cholera   dichotomy
    epoch   mechanic   orchestra   psychology technical
(f) chloride   chloroform chromium   chronicle   chrysalis

6.5   The letter <c> competes rather untidily with <s> as a spelling
of the phoneme /s/. There are homophones such as *cent – sent, cell
– sell, council – counsel*. What guidelines can help in choosing
between <s> and <c> spellings in the following words?

aerosol   atrocity bouncer   bus   conceive concept
curiosity dance   deceive   deception   decide   decisive
defiance   despot   diffidence dinosaur   disgust   dishonour
dismay   ecstasy   electricity else   epilepsy escape
exercise   fence   geneticist gipsy   heresy   hypocrisy
incise   jealousy license   master   mishap   misjudge
normalcy   once   persuade   pestilence practice procession
recede   receive   receptor   sample   scheme   secrecy
skin   slide   sphere   stay   suicide   tense

6.6 We have seen that <h> is used as an auxiliary letter to make up complex spellings such as <ch> *chin*, <sh> *shin*, <th> *thin*. What other consonant digraphs are formed with <h> in this way? What kinds of words do they occur in?

SUMMARY

■ In exploring divergent consonant spellings, letters may be roughly classified as empty <de**b**t>, inert <si**g**n> or auxiliary <**sh**ave> according to their role in the spelling of a particular word.

SOME VOWEL SPELLINGS

7

Divergence is particularly common with vowel spellings.

7.1 The irregularities of present-day English spelling are more in evidence with vowels than with consonants. The following minor correspondences are particularly troublesome. Try to find one or two examples of each.

1 \<aer\> ≡ /eə(r)/	2 \<augh\> ≡ /ɔː/	3 \<ah\> ≡ /ɑː/
4 \<al\> ≡ /ɑː/	5 \<eau\> ≡ /oʊ/	6 \<eigh\> ≡ /eɪ/
7 \<ei\> ≡ /iː/	8 \<eu\> ≡ /(j)uː/	9 \<ey\> ≡ /eɪ/
10 \<igh\> ≡ /aɪ/	11 \<oa\> ≡ /oʊ/	12 \<oir(e)\> ≡ /wɑː(r)/
13 \<oor\> ≡ /ɔː(r)/	14 \<oo\> ≡ /ʊ/	15 \<ough\> ≡ /ɔː/
16 \<ough\> ≡ /aʊ/	17 \<ough\> ≡ /ʌf/	18 \<ough\> ≡ /ɒf/, /ɑːf/
19 \<ough\> ≡ /uː/	20 \<ough\> ≡ /oʊ/	21 \<oul\> ≡ /ʊ/
22 \<our\> ≡ /aʊə(r)/	23 \<our\> ≡ /ʌr/	24 \<ui\> ≡ /uː/

7.2 How may a writer know how to spell the ending /oʊ/ in the following sample words? How do you decide between the spelling \<-o\> and \<-ow\>?

avocado	banjo	beano	cargo	casino	cello
echo	gusto	hero	judo	jumbo	kilo
mango	motto	negro	photo	salvo	solo
tango	tempo	torso	trio	veto	yobbo

arrow	barrow	bellow	borrow	burrow	elbow
fellow	follow	furrow	hollow	marrow	meadow
minnow	pillow	shadow	shallow	sorrow	sparrow
swallow	widow	willow	window	winnow	yellow

31

7.3   While discussing the ending <-o> ≡ /oʊ/, we can note that there is a measure of uncertainty how you form the plural. To which of the following words would you add <-es> rather than simple <-s> to form the plural? Is there any guideline to use?

boyo	bucko	cameo	cargo	commando	concerto
dipso	domino	go	halo	hero	indigo
mulatto	no	potato	quarto	radio	solo
soprano	tomato	tornado	torpedo	volcano	wino

SUMMARY

- Divergence in vowel spelling includes a large number of minor correspondences, which often occur in common words.
- The endings <-o> and <-ow> are predictable not only by origin, but by phonetic criteria.

LOOK-ALIKES AND SOUND-ALIKES

8

In any writing system that has evolved over a long period of time, you will find examples of:

- HOMOGRAPHS – words pronounced differently but written with the same spelling and
- HOMOPHONES – words pronounced the same but written with different spellings.

Homographs

Homophones

Both look-alikes (homographs) and sound-alikes (homophones) represent only a fraction of English vocabulary, since different words are normally required both to sound different and to look different. In theory, homographs may be a problem for the reader. In *The bass was remarkably good*, is <bass> a singer /beɪs/ or a fish /bæs/? Take the book title *Reading in Perspective*: is it about the town *Reading* /ˈredɪŋ/ or about literacy /ˈriːdɪŋ/? Conversely, homophones may be a problem for the listener and writer. In /ðə ˈbeɪs laɪn wəz ˈtuː ˈloʊ/ are we talking about a *bass* or a *base*? In practice, however, it is only very occasionally that homographs or homophones are likely to cause misunderstandings. Usually the meaning is apparent from the context. Homographs and homophones can safely exist because both spoken and written language have a high level of redundancy: there are more than enough clues to the meaning.

EXERCISES ✎

8.1 Distinguish two different grammatical structures that occur with each of the following groups of words written as homographs:

(a) aged, blessed, crooked, cursed, dogged, learned;
(b) analyses, axes, bases, ellipses;
(c) abuse, close, diffuse, excuse, house, use.

Discussion

Classification of homographs and homophones may seem trivial to a literate native speaker, but put yourself in the position of a foreign learner or someone learning to read and write.

(a) With some verbs the <-ed> form covers two different functions and pronunciations: *blessed* may be past tense or participle /blest/ (*I am blessed with a good appetite*) or adjectival /ˈblesɪd/ (*It was a blessed relief*). Cf. also: *They were dogged by bad luck* and *They showed dogged perseverance*.

(b) The ending <-es> may represent the normal noun plural /-ɪz/ or the Latinate plural /-iːz/ of singular nouns that end in /-ɪs/: *axes* may relate to *axe* as /ˈæksɪz/, or to *axis* as /ˈæksiːz/. Other examples are *bases* (from *base/basis*), *ellipses* (from *ellipse/ellipsis*).

(c) The ambiguity of <s> as a spelling of both /s/ and /z/ underlies homographs such as *abuse, close, diffuse, excuse, house, use*, in which the /s/ form is the noun or adjective and the /z/ form is the verb form of the same lexeme. *Refuse*, however, represents different lexemes /ˈrefjuːs/ 'rubbish' (noun) and /rɪˈfjuːz/ 'to deny, decline' (verb).

8.2 Check that each of the following is one of a pair of homographs as is *bass*, both 'singer' and 'fish'.

bow	buffet	invalid	lead	live	minute
putting	read	row	tear	wind	wound

Some homographs are also homophones: *flatter* ('fawn upon') is a single morpheme, *flatter* ('more flat') is a comparative adjective. Here, two clearly different lexical meanings sound the same and are spelt the same. These two-way identities are sometimes referred to
Homonyms   as HOMONYMS.

EXERCISE ✎

8.3 Distinguish at least two clearly different lexical meanings for the following homonyms.

bark	barrow	bellows	bound	cricket	fell
fine	firm	fit	flat	hail	hamper
last	leaves	mews	mould	pants	plane
quail	quarry	rest	rose	row	stable

Homophones in one accent may not be homophones in another. In AmE *hostel* and *hostile* are homophones pronounced /ˈhɑːstl/. In BrE *hostile* ends in /-aɪl/. Similarly, *barrage* represents /ˈbɑːrɪdʒ/ as 'dam' and /bəˈrɑːʒ/ as 'artillery fire' for AmE speakers, but for BrE speakers they are homophones as /ˈbærɑːʒ/. *Primer* represents /ˈpraɪmə(r)/ as 'paint' and /ˈprɪmə(r)/ as 'textbook' for AmE speakers, but for BrE speakers they are homophones as /ˈpraɪmə(r)/.

Two accents may differ in their range of phoneme contrasts and this inevitably produces homophones: *fair* and *fur* are homophones with the same vowel phoneme on Merseyside, but usually contrast as /eə(r)/ and /ɜː(r)/ otherwise. In AmE the short open back vowel /ɒ/ has lost its rounding and fallen in with /ɑː/ so that *balm* and *bomb* are homophones for most AmE speakers, but not usually in BrE. Scottish speakers do not usually have a difference of vowel length between the vowels in *dawn* and *don* (both with an /ɔ/) or *pool* and *pull* (both with an /u/).

Homophones may come about in one accent rather than another through general differences in the distribution of phonemes: *court* and *caught* are homophones in southern BrE as /kɔːt/ and so are *whacks* and *wax* as /wæks/. Neither are homophones in Scottish English or in AmE, where they are differentiated by the presence or absence of /r/ and of /h/.

EXERCISES ✎

8.4 Word forms with final /s/ or /z/ as a plural or a verb ending frequently form homophones with words in which the /s/ or /z/ is not a suffix, as, for instance, *bays – baize*. Find such a homophone for each of the following words. Some words will not provide examples in all accents.

brews	brows	chews	claws	cops
crews	days	flecks	flocks	frays
guys	knows	lacks	laps	links
pleas	prays	pries	quarts	rays
sighs	tacks	teas	treaties	whacks

8.5 Forms with final /t/ or /d/ as the past-tense ending also form homophones with words in which the /t/ or /d/ is not a suffix, as, for instance, *allowed – aloud*. Find such a homophone for each of the following words. Again, some examples will not provide homophones in all accents.

banned	bawled	billed	bowled	brayed	brewed
candied	chased	cowered	crewed	ducked	fined
guessed	mined	missed	mowed	mustered	owed
paced	packed	sighed	stayed	swayed	tacked
tied	towed	trussed	weighed	wheeled	whirred

8.6 Words with the suffix <-er> (with various meanings) may also form homophones with words in which there is not a free form with an added suffix, as, for instance, *sensor – censor*. Find such a homophone for each of the following words. Here, too, some examples will not provide homophones for all speakers.

boarder	bolder	dyer	fisher	fryer
grosser	hanger	higher	leaver	meatier
rigger	saver	seller	sucker	tenner

Other examples of two-morpheme and single-morpheme homo-phones are *bridal*, *bridle*; *chilly*, *chilli*; *lessen*, *lesson*.

In two-morpheme homophones there is often a difference in the location of the morpheme boundary: *tax* + {plural} and *taxi* + {plural} are both /ˈtæksɪz/ for some speakers (though as /ˈtæksɪz/ – /ˈtæksiːz/ not for others). Consider the following radio news item:

> Both parties are using /ˈtæksɪz/ to capture the floating voter.

Does this mean *taxis* or *taxes*?

Other examples are:

banded – bandied	eyelet – islet	fallacies – phalluses
leased – least	pitted – pitied	poses – posies
studded – studied	tided – tidied	verdure – verger

Though these may be homophones for some BrE speakers, pairs such as *tided* – *tidied* may be different for the growing number of speakers who have /iː/ rather than /ɪ/ in final open unstressed syllables: /ˈtaɪd+ɪd/ (or /+əd/) – /ˈtaɪdiː+d/.

In polysyllabic words homophones may result from the reduction of different underlying vowels to /ə/:

confirmation – conformation	interpellation – interpolation
literal – littoral	vacation – vocation
veracious – voracious	

Particularly where one of the words has an <o> spelling, careful speakers aware of the possible confusion may have an unreduced vowel (/veɪˈkeɪʃn/ ≠ /voʊˈkeɪʃn/, /veˈreɪʃəs/ ≠ /vɒˈreɪʃəs/) to main-tain the difference. Some broadcasters pronounce *guerrilla* with /e/, rather than the normal /ə/, in reporting events in Africa, where 'attacked by gorillas' is a remote, if unrealistic, possibility.

Phonetic reductions that might cause confusion in the weak forms of function words are avoided. The preposition *on* does not usually reduce to /ən/ because of possible confusion with *and* in a phrase such as /ən ðə ˈteɪbl/. However, it does not matter that both the auxiliaries *is* and *has* are homophones when reduced to /s/ or /z/, since the verb form that follows is distinctive: /s/ in *Jack's gone*, *Jack's going*, /z/ in *Jill's gone*, *Jill's going*. Context should also distin-guish *there*, *their* and *they're*, but in practice these three are frequently mis-spelt.

8.7 Homophones may come about in non-rhotic accents simply because /r/ has been lost in one of the words, finally or before a consonant. Such a pair would not be homophones in rhotic accents, since one word would have /r/ and the other not. So in AmE or Scottish and Irish English *alms* and *arms* are not homophones. Non-rhotic accents will have homophones for the following words with a letter <r> in the spelling. Give examples.

alms	area	awe	bawd	beta	calve
caught	caulk	cause	cawed	cheetah	coma
cornea	curricula	father	flaw	formally	fought
lava	law	manna	nebula	panda	paw
peninsula	raw	rota	sauce	saw	schema
sought	spa	stalk	talk	tuba	uvula

8.8 Some homophones result from an empty letter in correspondences such as <kn> ≡ /n/, <wh> ≡ /w/, <wh> ≡ /h/, <wr> ≡ /r/, <gu> ≡ /g/ and <mb> ≡ /m/. The <wh> words will not form homophones in all accents. Note the homophones that lack the empty letter of the following words.

knave	knead	knew	knight	knot	know
whale	wheel	whether	which	while	whine
whither	whole	wrap	wreak	wreck	wrest
wretch	wright	write	wring	wrote	wrung
gauge	guild	guilt	climb	jamb	plumb

The <n> in *dam*, *damn* and the <g> in *sine*, *sign* are inert rather than empty letters: they have a phoneme correspondence in *damnation*, *signature*.

8.9 Homophones are frequently found with variant vowel spellings. Particularly common are homophones with the long vowels /iː, ɪə, eɪ, eə, aɪ, oʊ, ɔː/. Together they account for well over a hundred homophone pairs. Suggest a suitable homophone for each of the following words. Some may not provide homophones in all accents of English. Due to a transitional [ə] glide between /aɪ/ and a following 'dark' /l/, some speakers do not distinguish *file*, *phial* or *vile*, *vial*. This was the basis for a slogan protesting against a new airport runway at Styal, Cheshire: 'A new runway is not our Styal.'

/iː/ beach, sealing, creek, discrete, heel, meat, piece, suite.

/ɪə/ beer, deer, hear, peer, tier.

/eə/ bare, fair, flair, hare, pare, stair, their.

/aɪ/ dye, giro, lyre, sight, sleight, style, tire.

/oʊ/ groan, lode, lone, row, road, roll, sew, sole, toe, yolk.

/ɔː/ aural, fourth, hoard, horse, course, worn, ball, haul, mall, nought.

Other long vowels provide fewer examples:

/aʊ/ bough, fowl, flower.
/ɑː/ heart, balmy.
/uː/ pleural, route, troop, through.
/juː/ dew, hue, revue.
/ɜː/ birth, fur, heard, pearl, surf, turn, whirl, earn.

Homophones involving spelling variation in short vowels are much less common than with long vowels. The reason is that the short vowels have been subject to less phonetic change over the centuries and the spelling has remained fairly stable. Examples:

/e/ bread, bred; lead, led; leant, lent; read, red.
/ʌ/ none, nun; one, won; rough, ruff; ton, tun.
/ɒ/ swat, swot.

Though, as we have seen, most homophone pairs only differ in a vowel spelling or a consonant spelling, there are more complex differences:

choir – quire	choler – collar	colonel – kernel
cue – queue	genes – jeans	geezer – geyser
key – quay	mare – mayor	profit – prophet
raiser – razor	cymbal – symbol	gorilla – guerrilla

Homophones in figurative language for which there is no clear derivation often generate a great deal of speculation. Is it to be *hair-brained* or *hare-brained*? **Hair-lip* is a misunderstanding of the simile in *hare-lip*. Similarly, do we leave the *fairway* or *fareway*? In spite of associations with *fare* in the sense of 'travel' and compounds such as *wayfarer*, *thoroughfare*, most dictionaries prefer *fairway*.

Identity or near-identity of sound or spelling has long been exploited for stylistic purposes. Puns have to run the risk of not being noticed, so near-identity often serves very well in slapstick comedy:

ANTONY: These desert nomads are intense lovers.
CAESAR: Of course. They do everything in tents.

Here there is only a strict homophone for those who do not contrast /nts/ and /ns/ *as in a pound of mints/mince*, but have /nts/ for both.

EXERCISE ✎

8.10 The following word pairs have each developed from variant spellings of what was once the same word. Some, such as <kerb>/<curb> are homophones, but others, such as <price>/<prize> have different pronunciations. Some pairs represent an earlier and a later borrowing from French, such as <artist>/<artiste>. The later borrowing often has final stress as a marker of its Frenchness.

Use a large dictionary and your own insight to explain how the following pairs now differ in meaning. Three examples are commented on below to show you the kind of information you can find.

artist – artiste	block – bloc	borne – born
broach – brooch	canvas – canvass	check – cheque
chord – cord	discreet – discrete	draught – draft
faint – feint	flower – flour	human – humane
license – licence	lightening – lightning	local – locale
mantle – mantel	metal – mettle	of – off
patron – pattern	person – parson	plain – plane
plait – pleat	premise – premiss	price – prize
queue – cue	review – revue	rout – route
set – sett	shagreen – chagrin	stanch – staunch
temper – tamper	tire – tyre	ton – tun
troop – troupe	urban – urbane	whisky – whiskey

Examples

courtesy – curtsy: the informal pronunciation as two syllables /'kɜː(r)tsɪ/ with the spelling *curtsy* means a courteous greeting.

critic /'krɪtɪk/ – *critique* /krɪ'tiːk/: the spelling *critic* was originally used for both the person and the critical essay. The French spelling *critique*, with final stress, came in as an eighteenth-century differentiation of the two.

curb – kerb: this is one of the neatest examples of differentiation: *kerb* in BrE has the specialised sense of a stone edging to a pavement. The <curb> spelling is still used for both in AmE. An American street sign misunderstood by British visitors is *Curb your dog!*, where *curb* means 'take to the kerb', not 'restrain'.

SUMMARY

- Homographs are difficult for the reader and homophones for the writer, though the context almost always points to the right choice.
- Variant spellings of the same word, such as *human – humane*, *curb – kerb*, have often taken on quite different meanings over the centuries.

9 SOUND-ALIKE AFFIXES

Some of the commonest spelling mistakes involve homophonous affixes. These include the following:

(a) <-ant/-ent>, <-ance/-ence>, <-ancy/-ency>;
(b) <-able>, <-ible> in adjectives;
(c) <-er>, <-or> in agent nouns;
(d) stressed <-eer>, <-ier> in agent nouns;
(e) stressed <-ette>, <-et> in nouns;
(f) <-ice>, <-is> in nouns;
(g) <-ise>, <-ize> in verbs;
(h) the prefixes <en-> and <in->.

Affixes themselves are often homophones and are a frequent source of spelling mistakes. Since the difference between the opposite meanings 'out' and 'in' is not reflected in the pronunciation of *eruption* and *irruption* as /ɪˈrʌpʃn/, we have all the ingredients for confusion as in:

the *eruption of our hero *into this strange new world

It is no trouble at all, in the text-to-speech direction, for the reader to know that both *sequence* and *substance* are pronounced with the same ending /-ən(t)s/. It is more difficult, working in the speech-to-text direction, to spell such a suffix. In this section we shall examine some of the more common affix confusions.

To some extent the spelling of an affix will be evident from meaning, or from grammatical function or from related forms. The words *hydrometer* and *arbiter* both end in /-ɪtə(r)/. Anyone who can associate *hydrometer* with 'measuring' and *meter* is not likely to write *<hydromiter>.

The words *physician* and *repetition* both end in /-ɪʃn/. The <-ician> spelling occurs when the referent is a 'human, professional' noun:

mathematician, optician, phonetician, politician, technician. More-over, anyone who associates *technician* with the /k/ of *technical, technique* or its AmE spelling *technic*, is not likely to write *<technition>.

An awareness of word structure and derivations clearly plays an important role in selecting the correct spelling when pronunciation alone is not decisive.

This is a notorious source of mis-spellings in present-day English because the vowel in both sets of suffixes is reduced to /ə/. There is some guidance on the choice of <a> or <e> spellings from related forms with a stressed vowel: *consequent – consequential; substance – substantial*. All three endings <-ant>, <-ance>, <-ancy> or <-ent>, <-ence>, <-ency> may occur, but sometimes there are gaps: we have *different, difference*, but rarely *differency*; we have *delinquent, delinquency*, but rarely *delinquence*.

<-A/ENT>,
<-A/ENCE>,
<-A/ENCY>

Words with these suffixes often came into English by way of French, where the Latin derivation <-ent> may have been changed into <-ant>. Some English writers loyal to Latin, however, wanted an <e> spelling in words such as *dependent* (from Latin *pendere*). So for some words, dictionary makers have over the years allowed both spellings. Nowadays, *dependence* and *dependency* are the norm, though before 1800 *dependance, dependancy* were also found. The adjective is usually *dependent*, but the noun may be either *a dependent* or *a dependant*. With the same root, *a pendant* is the noun and *pendent* the adjective.

To allow free variation like this in some words, but not in others, only serves to confuse spellers still further. Webster's *Third New International Dictionary* (1961, p. 25a) estimates degrees of variability in spelling as follows, but it hardly inspires confidence in the speller:

- 'almost always' spelt so are *ascendant, attendance, descendant, intendant, pendant* (noun), *dependency, dependent* (adj.), *tendency, transcendent, superintendent*;
- 'usually' spelt so are *expellant, propellant, impellent, repellent*;
- 'about equally' spelt with <a>/<e> are *ascendancy, dependant* (noun), *pendant* (adj.), which means, of course, 'take your pick'.

EXERCISES ✎

9.1 This exercise will familiarise you with <-e->-spelt suffixes attached to bound forms. Go through the following list making up words ending in <-ent>, <-ence> or <-ency>:

abhorr-	abs-	abstin-	ambi-	anci-	ard-
audi-	belliger-	cad-	clem-	cli-	compet-
complac-	congru-	consci-	constitu-	contin-	conveni-
cred-	dec-	decad-	delinqu-	depend-	deterg-

deterr-	dilig-	ebulli-	eloqu-	emin-	ess-
excell-	exist-	expedi-	experi-	ferv-	frequ-
imman-	immin-	impud-	inadvert-	innoc-	instrum-
intellig-	intermitt-	intransig-	lat-	leni-	neglig-
obedi-	omnisci-	pat-	pati-	penit-	perman-
pestil-	pres-	preval-	promin-	prud-	pung-
rec-	reg-	repell-	resili-	resplend-	rever-
sali-	sent-	senti-	sil-	string-	strid-
tang-	tend-	transi-	urg-	vehem-	viol-

9.2   This exercise makes you choose. Supply the missing letter <a> or <e> in the following words.

abund*nce	adher*nt	anteced*nt	benign*nt
blat*nt	brilli*nt	clairvoy*nt	compon*nt
confid*nce	consequ*nce	consist*ncy	coven*nt
disson*nt	diverg*nt	domin*nce	dorm*nt
evid*nce	exorbit*nt	extravag*nt	exuber*nt
flamboy*nt	hesit*nt	immigr*nt	incess*nt
incid*nt	indulg*nt	influ*nce	insolv*ncy
insurg*nt	itiner*nt	jubil*nt	lubric*nt
malign*nt	mut*nt	petul*nt	preponder*nt
recipi*nt	recumb*nt	recurr*nt	redol*nt
redund*ncy	refer*nce	relev*nce	resid*nce
stimul*nt	transpar*nt	vali*nt	vigil*nt

<-ABLE>, <-IBLE> IN ADJECTIVES

These endings are also a disaster area. The productive suffix is <-able>. It can be added to any vaguely transitive verb (one that can have an 'object' for the action of the verb): *actable, awakenable, bemoanable, chattable, crammable, dethronable, garbleable, kissable, trafficable*, etc. – all from *OED*. Occasionally, <-able> is added to a noun such as *marriageable, peaceable*, but this is quite exceptional for <-ible>: *contemptible*.

EXERCISE ✎

9.3   There are exceptions to only having <-able> after a free form. Some words, like *accessible*, have <-ible> after a free form instead. These tend to have a final /d/, /t/ or /s/ and occasionally /n/ before the suffix. Suggest some examples.

The choice between <-able> and <-ible> is often a matter of controversy. Some words, such as *tenable*, have come into English by way of French, where many Latin <i> forms have been standardised on <-able>. While English has *responsible*, French has *responsable*.

If the stem is phonetically an English free-form verb, it is fairly safe to use <-able>: *admittable, comprehendable, defendable, dividable, permittable, reprehendable, transmittable*. A bound verb stem with the same lexeme generally requires <-ible>: *admissible, comprehensible, defensible, divisible, extensible, permissible, reprehensible, transmissible*.

Usage is not always consistent. Some dictionaries allow either <-able> or <-ible> in *collapsible, collectible, comprehendible, discernible, expressible, extendible, gullible, perfectible*.

One group of words with <-able> after a bound form are *abominable, appreciable, calculable, demonstrable, educable, equable, palpable*, where the related verb ends in <-ate> as *appreciate, educate*, or where there is a noun in <-ation> as *durable – duration*. Other instances of <-able> after a bound form are *amiable, capable, despicable*.

Words which have <-ible> after a bound form include:

audible	compatible	corrigible	credible	edible
eligible	fallible	feasible	horrible	intelligible
invincible	legible	negligible	ostensible	plausible
possible	susceptible	tangible	terrible	visible

An <e> is naturally kept before the ending when it marks a particular consonant, as in <(d)ge> ≡ /dʒ/, <ce> ≡ /s/: *bridgeable, changeable, gaugeable, serviceable*.

There is some variability in the elision of final <e> in the stem: *bribeable – bribable, blameable – blamable, chaseable – chasable, moveable – movable, solveable – solvable, unmistakeable – unmistakable*, etc. *OED* (under -*able*) comments: 'As much reason can be given and as much authority cited for one spelling as the other, and until a reform of English spelling is made, the double form of these words must continue.' Stem-final <-y> becomes <i> before <-able> as in: *dutiable, enviable, reliable*, but not when the <y> is an auxiliary letter in a vowel spelling: *assayable, enjoyable*. Exceptions are *flyable, fryable* (from *fry*; cf. *friable* 'crumbly').

Agent nouns represent the 'doer' of an action. At first sight the difference between <-er> and <-or> in agent nouns formed from verbs is one between native words with <-er> and Latinate words with <-or>, but the distribution of the two forms is more complicated and by no means fully regular or consistent.

**<-ER>, <-OR>
IN AGENT
NOUNS**

EXERCISE ✎

9.4 Supply the missing letter <o> or <e> in the endings of the following words.

adapt*r	agitat*r	alternat*r	astronom*r	atomis*r
barrist*r	chorist*r	commut*r	condens*r	congen*r

constrict*r   curat*r   deposit*r   detect*r   elevat*r
geograph*r   improvis*r   inhibit*r   insulat*r   liquefi*r
predecess*r   rotat*r   spectat*r   subscrib*r   tut*r

<-EER>, <-IER> IN AGENT NOUNS

EXERCISE

9.5 The suffixes <-eer> amd <-ier> are found in nouns denoting human agents. Supply the missing letter <i> or <e> in the following words.

auction*er   bombard*er   brigad*er   buccan*er   cash*er
engin*er   gondol*er   grenad*er   mountain*er mutin*er
pamphlet*er profit*er   racket*er   sonnet*er   volunt*er

<-ETTE>, <-ET> IN NOUNS

The ending <-ette>, found largely in loan-words from French, usually retains a primary stress. Sometimes it is added to a bound stem, *cassette*, sometimes to a free stem, *rosette*.

brunette   cassette   coquette   corvette   courgette
gazette   kitchenette laundrette maisonette   marionette
novelette   pipette   pirouette   rosette   roulette
serviette   silhouette   statuette   suffragette usherette

The stress may shift to the first syllable in one or two words, such as *cigarette*, *etiquette*. The word *omelette* (or *omelet*) is quite exceptional in that the stress is never on the last syllable and the vowel of that syllable is reduced to /ə/ or /ɪ/ as /ˈɒmlət/, /ˈɒmlɪt/.

Purists object to unrestricted use of <-ette> after any minimal free form: 'most of these, as *leaderette*, *sermonette*, *essayette*, can scarcely be said to be in good use' (*OED*, under *-ette*). Since then the public has been offered *lecturette*, *luncheonette*, *roomette*, and worse. Coinages such as *hackette* 'woman journalist' or *farmerette* are demeaning to women, combining as they do 'little' + 'feminine'.

Words spelt with final <-et> include

cadet   clarinet   duet   epaulet   martinet   minuet
octet   quartet   quintet sextet   septet   stockinet

Alternative spellings *quartette* and *quintette* sometimes occur. *Stockinet*, an elastic cotton fabric, comes from a fusing of *stocking net*.

9.6 There are other stressed endings which have a <-VCCe> pattern, but with consonant letters other than <-ette>, usually from French. Suggest some such words, e.g. *giraffe*, *largesse*.

<-ICE>, <-IS> IN NOUNS

9.7 The ending <-ice> comes through French from a number of Latin origins. Apart from being a marker of nouns, it has no particular consistent meaning. On the other hand, if you can recognise Greek elements in a word, you will know that it has the ending <-is>. Supply the ending <-ice> or <-is> to complete the following nouns.

accompl*	acropol*	analys*	antithes*	apprent*
armist*	avar*	benef*	bod*	bronchit*
cannab*	chal*	copp*	corn*	coward*
crev*	dentifr*	diagnos*	dialys*	edif*
emphas*	epiderm*	genes*	hosp*	jaund*
just*	latt*	liquor*	mal*	metropol*
nemes*	nov*	orif*	paralys*	parenthes*
poult*	pract*	precip*	prejud*	synthes*

<-ISE>, <-IZE> IN VERBS

9.8 You will probably have noticed that there are varying conventions about the spelling of verbs ending in /-aɪz/. Should the ending be spelt <-ise> or <-ize>? There are three alternative conventions in use. Which do you use?

    (a) baptize, decimalise, supervise;
    (b) baptize, decimalize, supervise;
    (c) baptise, decimalise, supervise.

Discussion

Convention (a) is very scholarly and uses the <-ize> spelling in words, such as *baptize*, *agonize*, which represent actual Greek verbs. There are also words that have been made up in later Latin or in French to imitate Greek (*humanise*), or within English itself (*decimalise*, *bowdlerise*). These are given the different spelling <-ise>.

Some traditional British publishers adopt this purist approach and spell the two groups differently. That is thoroughly confusing for the ordinary speller. The word *supervise* ends in a Latin root <-vis(e)> 'look', as in *supervision* ('looking over') and cannot be spelt with *<-ize>.

Convention (b) is the standard spelling in the United States, but is also used by some British publishers. Convention (c) is favoured by other British publishers who make the <s> spelling standard, as French has done. To standardise on a <z> spelling for this verb ending, as AmE spelling has done, has disadvantages, because there are a number of Latinate verbs ending in <-ise> which have historically nothing to do with this suffix:

advertise	apprise	circumcise	comprise	compromise
despise	devise	excise	exercise	improvise
incise	revise	supervise	surmise	surprise

If you make <baptize>, <decimalize> the standard spelling, you are likely to get a wayward *<supervize>. *OED* argues that the pronunciation is /z/ and that this justifies the <z> spelling. But this ignores the fact that <s> ≡ /z/ happens to be the commonest spelling of /z/ overall. Moreover, if the suffix <-ism> is the overall standard for nouns formed from such verbs, as in *baptism*, *organism*, why not have <-ise> as the verb ending?

THE PREFIXES <EN->, <IN->

The unstressed prefixes <en-> and <in-> (both meaning 'in') are often mere variants. The <en-> spelling supposedly occurs in words which have come from Latin through French and the <in-> spelling for words direct from Latin. In practice, this criterion is not much use to the average speller.

Some speakers, often in the north of England, tend to have a spelling pronunciation <en-> ≡ /en/ rather than /ɪn/, which largely does away with the problem. Indeed it is quite common practice to have a formal pronunciation /en-/ for literary words such as *engender*.

With some words there is a choice. The following words may have either <en-> or <in->, but with no difference in use: *enclose, encrust, endorse, enfold, engrain, engraft, entrench, entrust, entwine.*

The following is a sample of purely <en-> words with free stems:

enable	enact	encamp	enchant	encircle
encounter	encourage	endanger	endear	enfeeble
enfranchise	engrossed	enjoy	enlarge	enlist
enliven	ennoble	enrage	entangle	entomb

With bound stems there are: *encroach, endeavour, endorse, endow, enhance, entice*, etc.

9.9 Do you think that there is any difference of meaning between *enquire*, *enquiry* and *inquire*, *inquiry*, assuming that you would use both spellings? Can you tie this difference to particular contexts? Similarly, is there any difference between *ensure* and *insure*?

SUMMARY

- Some of the commonest spelling mistakes involve confusion of homophonous endings, such as <-ant>/<-ent> *reluctant – translucent*, <-able>/<-ible> *demonstrable – discernible*. In many cases usage varies and there are few firm guidelines.

10 THE SPELLING OF NAMES

> Family names are like totems. If your name is *Thynne*, the irregularity in spelling is a family heirloom. Padding with empty letters is common in family names to give them bulk. In trademarks irregularity is deliberately exploited to stake out a commercial identity. Place-names that have become worn down over the centuries in local use are often given a new, more regular spelling pronunciation by outsiders.

'How do you spell your name?' is a question which implies that we have some freedom. Yet it also implies that nowadays people are expected to keep to one particular variant of their name all the time. In earlier centuries people could and did write their own name differently from occasion to occasion. We are all aware of the range of conventional spellings of family names. A person answering to /ˈgɪlmɔː(r)/ may spell it *Gilmore* or *Gilmour*; /liː/ may be spelt *Lea*, *Lee* or *Leigh*; /ˈgreɪndʒə(r)/ may be spelt *Grainger* or *Granger*, and so on.

A spelling which looks old and is notably out of step with present-day spelling conventions shows that the family is 'old', in the sense of having a long recorded history. Particularly prestigious are names that preserve Norman-French spellings, such as *Beaulieu* /ˈbjuːlɪ/, since these are both old and aristocratic. The Marquis of Cholmondeley, whose name is /ˈtʃʌmlɪ/, probably has the ultimate Norman totem, closely challenged by native Anglo-Saxon *Featherstonehaugh*, now pronounced /ˈfænʃɔː/, or *Woolfardsworthy*, pronounced /ˈwʊlzərɪ/.

EXERCISE ✎

10.1 There is much less variation in the spelling of first names, but here are some for which you will know an alternative spelling:

Alan	Anthony	Brian	Caroline	Catherine	Elisabeth
Jeffrey	John	Lewis	Linda	Marian	Marjorie

It is only to be expected that foreign names such as *Reykjavik*, *Phnom Penh*, *Vosges*, *Schwyz*, *Mmabatho*, *Ljubljana* will be difficult for both reader and writer to match up to English spelling conventions. Some foreign names have acquired both an anglicised spelling and pronunciation. *Livorno*, *Moskva*, *Köbenhavn* have become *Leghorn*, *Moscow*, *Copenhagen*.

If you take a foreign spelling and simply match the letters with a string of native English conventions, then you have a SPELLING PRONUNCIATION. Foreign place-names borrowed in the United States for new settlements usually have a spelling pronunciation: *Cairo* as /ˈkeɪroʊ/ not /ˈkaɪəroʊ/, *Lima* in Ohio as /ˈlaɪmə/ not /ˈliːmə/, *Edinburgh* in Texas as /ˈednbɜː(r)ɡ/ not /ˈednbərə/, *Madras* in Oregon as /ˈmædrəs/ not /məˈdræs/, *Milan* in Indiana as /ˈmɪlən/ not /mɪˈlæn/, *Valois* in New York state as /vəˈlɔɪs/ not /vælˈwɑː/ (*LPD*).

Names do not have to be foreign to be difficult. It is not by any means obvious to strangers that *Hawick* is pronounced /hɔɪk/ by those who know the place, or that a place referred to as /hɔɪk/ is *Hawick* on the signposts. No stranger, reading the place-name *Keighley*, could guess that it is /ˈkiːθlɪ/, or hearing the place-name /ˈheɪzbərə/ could possibly imagine that the spelling was *Happisburgh*.

Variants of complex names may come about when the structure of the name ceases to be obvious. Spellings with <x> may obscure such a boundary in *Dixon*, *Nixon*, *Hauxwell*, which are opaque compared with *Dickson*, 'son of Dick', *Nickson*, *Hawkswell*. *Dixon* has the spelling of a single morpheme, as does *tax* compared with *tacks*.

Spelling pronunciation

EXERCISE ✎

10.2 How does the spelling of the following family names differ from that of ordinary words? What spelling conventions are ignored?

Aske	Bigge	Boycott	Crowe	Donne	Hayter
Hobbes	Lippincott	Powicke	Symons	Thorne	Wynne

This is an exercise that you can extend for yourself by browsing through the telephone directory on the look-out for irregularities.

Foreign names ending in <-e> may be a problem for the reader. Is final <-e> just an empty letter, or a long vowel marker, or does it represent a separate vowel, as does <e> ≡ /ə/ in *Isolde*, or <e> ≡ /ɪ/ in *Iolanthe*? *Metropole* /ˈmetrəpoʊl/ can conceivably be misread as */meˈtrɒpəlɪ/ on the lines of *metropolis* /meˈtrɒpəlɪs/. Some names have two pronunciations: *Eunice* as /ˈjuːnɪs/ or /juːˈnaɪsɪ/, *Irene* as /ˈaɪəriːn/ or /aɪˈriːnɪ/, *Rhode* as /roʊd/ or /ˈroʊdɪ/.

NAME SHORTENING

Abbreviated names do not usually have <C>-doubling, since any extra letters would be at odds with the shortening: *Bob, Dan, Don, Fred, Gus, Ken, Meg, Pam, Tim*, etc. So we have *Reg* not <Redge>, *Sol* not <Soll>. Consequently, forms such as *Robb, Watt* are marked by the <C>-doubling as surnames rather than first names. If the form is not simply a shortening, but has some other alteration as well, there may be conventional doubling. Compare the simple abbreviations *Liz, Vic*, with *Bess* (*Elizabeth*), *Dick* (*Richard*), *Mick* (*Michael*), *Nick* (*Nicholas*).

EXERCISES ✎

10.3   There are sometimes social reasons for avoiding the normal pronunciation or spelling of a name. Some names have unpleasant or embarrassing associations. How do you account for the pronunciation by careful owners of the following names?

Astle /ˈæstl/ (not /ˈɑːsl/ as in *castle*); Belcher with /ʃ/ not /tʃ/; Bottome /bəˈtoʊm/; Buggs /bjuːgz/; Fudge /fjuːdʒ/; Poe /poʊɪ/; DeAth /diːˈæθ/; Uranus /ˈjʊərənəs/.

10.4   Here are ten favourite women's names and ten favourite men's names. They came top in a poll of the most feminine and the most masculine names. Do you notice any phonetic differences between the two groups? How do these differences tie in with the stereotyping of 'feminine' and 'masculine'?

(You could use some simple phonetic categories here as part of your analysis: the consonants /p, b, t, d, k, g, tʃ, dʒ/ are called 'stops' because the air flow through the mouth is blocked for a fraction of a second; consonants other than stops are 'continuants'.)

Diana	Elizabeth	Emily	Emma	Katherine
Lucy	Mary	Rose	Sophie	Victoria
David	Edward	James	John	Mark
Matthew	Michael	Paul	Peter	Richard

By all means repeat the exercise with any random sample of women's and men's names, preferably larger than this.

10.5   Trade and product names deliberately flout spelling conventions in the search for a unique name. What irregularities are exploited in the following trade names? Find some trade name examples of your own in advertisements and shops and explain the mis-spellings.

Glyd-Tracc	Kleen-Shyne	Kul Ryde
Kwik-Pak	Likker Pikker	Olde Tyme Fayre
Pollon Eze	Serve-u-Rite	Spud-u-Like

Discussion

Respelling of /k/ is a clear favourite. There is a general assumption that <k> is a 'natural' spelling of /k/, just as <z> for /z/, rather than the commoner <s>. The single-letter spellings <k> and <z> can only represent phonemes /k/ and /z/ regardless of context. The two different letters of doubled <ck> are often changed to a doubled *<cc> or *<kk>. Also common are irregular <y> spellings of /aɪ/: *<Shyne>, *<Ryde>, and variant spellings of an /ə/: *<Pollon>.

Letters, often capitals, are sometimes intended to be read as the name of the letter – <u> to represent *you* /juː/: *<Spud-u-Like> ('a baked potato shop') or *<Serve-u-Rite> ('a delivery service').

Many trade names and slogans have become institutionalised spelling mistakes: *<Beanz meanz Heinz>.

10.6 How would you pronounce the following names of places in England if you were an outsider who had never come across them before?

Almondsbury	Barnoldswick	Bicester	Burwash
Cirencester	Congresbury	Darwen	Daventry
Hunstanton	Leominster	Puncknowle	Rothwell
Salkeld	Sawbridgeworth	Slaithwaite	Uttoxeter

Discussion

It may come as a surprise to see how worn-down their traditional local pronunciations have become with the passage of time. Traditional local pronunciations are as follows:

Almondsbury /ˈeɪmzbrɪ/	Barnoldswick /ˈbɑːlɪk/
Bicester /ˈbɪstə(r)/	Burwash /ˈbʌrəs/
Cirencester /ˈsɪsɪstə(r)/	Congresbury /ˈkuːmzbrɪ/
Darwen /ˈdærən/	Daventry /ˈdeɪntrɪ/
Hunstanton /ˈhʌnstən/	Leominster /ˈlemstə(r)/
Puncknowle/ˈpʌnl/	Rothwell /ˈrouəl/
Salkeld /ˈsæfld/	Sawbridgeworth /ˈsæpswə(r)θ/
Slaithwaite /ˈslauɪt/	Uttoxeter /ˈʌksɪtə(r)/

Consonant clusters are simplified and unstressed syllables are often lost. This wearing down of a place-name by frequent local use is similar to the reduced forms of words found in jargons. In nautical jargon the terms *foresail, forecastle, foremast* are /ˈfɔː(r)sl/, /ˈfouksl/ and /ˈfɔː(r)məst/, with reduced forms for *sail, castle* and *mast*.

Strangers will naturally attempt a spelling pronunciation of a reduced place-name, and this outsider's alternative may come to be regarded as an 'educated' pronunciation. Cirencester and Uttoxeter locals may have a guilty feeling that they ought really to be saying /ˈsaɪərənsestə(r)/ and /juːˈtɒksɪtə(r)/. Alternatively, a worn-down name may be respelt and its original reference lost. Churchdown near Gloucester came to be pronounced /ˈtʃɜː(r)zdən/, which was reinterpreted as /ˈtʃouzn/, a pronunciation that survives in Chosen Hill.

Some insecurity attaches to the pronunciation of English place-names. Analogy is never quite safe. Places containing initial <Hey-> are usually pronounced /heɪ-/ *Heycock*, *Heyno*, *Heytesbury*, *Heywood*; but *Heysham* has /hiː-/. The element {holy} has an unshortened vowel /ˈhoʊlɪ-/ in *Holycross*, *Holyoake* but a shortened vowel /ˈhɒlɪ-/ in *Holyhead*, *Holyrood*, *Holywell*.

SUMMARY

- Personal names, trademarks and place-names show considerable irregularity in spelling. This is often deliberately contrived and may serve a useful 'distinctive' purpose.

RULES AND MISTAKES

11

People like to think of the ability to spell as rule-governed. A spelling mistake seems to imply a broken rule. But ask someone to give you examples of spelling rules and they will soon falter. Anyone who is literate will probably have long forgotten the structured way in which they were taught to read and write.

In a strictly alphabetic system, there would be no divergence. You would find a regular one-to-one correspondence between each phoneme and its spelling. This is certainly not so for correspondences in English. The nearest we get to it is perhaps /h/ ≡ <h>, as in *hat*. Even this assumes that we are dealing with the <wh> of *who*, the <sh> of *shop*, the <th> of *think*, etc. as independent complex units of spelling. In so far as we can describe English spelling conventions as a set of correspondences, we are using correspondence 'rules'.

Some correspondences are restricted to particular contexts. Since <C>-doubling occurs after a short stressed vowel, we can find a word spelt <tack> but never one spelt *<ckat>. Another correspondence rule for a particular context is:

'<ig> ≡ /aɪ/ before final <m, n>' (*design, paradigm*)

People seem reluctant to call such statements 'rules'. But if you set out to write computer programs to turn written words into phonemes (text-to-speech) or phonemes into written text (speech-to-text), you would be writing CORRESPONDENCE RULES like these. The public, however, takes correspondence rules for granted and looks to memorable little jingles to safeguard against common errors.

CORRESPON-DENCES

Correspondence rules

53

REFERENCE RULES

11.1 Ask people to give you one or two examples of spelling rules that they are familiar with. Write down exactly what your informants say and test the rules to see if they are fully explicit. If you applied the rules mechanically, would they work?

Discussion

The results of such an enquiry are fairly predictable. You will probably be offered:

1 '<i> before <e> except after <c>', referring to *field*, *receive*,

or perhaps:

2 'alter <-y> to <-ie> before adding <s>', referring to *orgy*, *orgies*, *deny*, *denies*.

Reference rules

These can be called REFERENCE RULES, since they are memorable and you have them to refer to when you are hesitant about a particular spelling.

The more closely one looks at rule (1), the more peculiar it seems. It helps to decide between /iː/ ≡ <ie> in *believe*, etc. and /iː/ ≡ <ei> in *deceive*, etc. These <ie> and <ei> spellings of /iː/ are a visual switching round (metathesis) of each other. The rule does not, however, apply to phonemes other than /iː/. Although *seize* , *seizure* are exceptions to the rule, *heifer* with /e/ ≡ <ei> or *rein*, *vein* with /eɪ/ ≡ <ei> have nothing to do with it. The letters <ie> are not a usual spelling of the phoneme /e/ (in spite of *friend*) or of /eɪ/. The variable pair *either* and *neither*, which usually have /aɪ/ in BrE and /iː/ in AmE, are outside the rule. In AmE *leisure* with /iː/ is an exception; in BrE with /e/ it is outside the scope of the rule. The rule is quite unreliable with names: *Dalgleish, Feilden, Keith, Leigh, Monteith, MacNeice, Neil, Reid*, etc.

A more adequate, but less memorable wording of rule (1) would be:

'In spelling an invariable /iː/ with the letters <i> and <e>, the <i> goes before the <e> except after <c>.'

Graphotactic rules

This rule can also be classified as a GRAPHOTACTIC RULE (or 'letter-distribution rule') which restricts possible letter sequences. Not all such rules are easily stated as quotable reference rules. For instance, it is part of your competence as a speller to know that words do not end in <j>, <q>, <u>, <v> or a single <z> unless they are distinctly foreign, as in *raj, Iraq, guru, fez*, or slang, as in *spiv, baz*. True as this may be, it is hardly quotable as a reference rule.

Graphotactic rules may have explanatory value in laying bare some of the general design principles. There is the so-called 'short word rule', which provides a minimum bulk of three letters for lexical words as opposed to function words (p. 76). The rules for <e>-marking of long vowels and <C>-doubling as a marking of short vowels have graphotactic complications. They depend on whether the vowel in question is spelt by one or more letters: we have <bedding> but not *<headding>, <grate> but not *<greate> (p. 18).

Let us return to our search for other quotable reference rules. One rule you are likely to be offered is (2). It reminds you that the plural of *army, penny, sky*, is *armies, pennies, skies*, not *<armys>, etc. and that you have the verb form *envies, marries, relies*, not *<envys>, etc. Here, too, you have to be careful of the wording of the rule. The <-y> should not be part of a complex spelling <oy>, <ay>, <ey>, as in *employs, relays, obeys*, not *<emploies>, etc. The added <s> should not be the possessive, as in *Tommy's, anybody's*. The apostrophe shows that these are not plural forms.

The letter <-y> is generally used as a word-final variant of the letter <i>. If you add a suffix to a word ending in <-y>, the <-y> usually 'changes' to <i>, as in:

contrariwise	defiant	dutiful	fanciful	happiness
hardihood	kindliness	livelihood	merrily	merriment
penniless	pitiless	reliance	wearily	wearisome

The change applies before <-ed>, as in *defied, pitied*, but not before <-ing>: *defying, pitying*, since a sequence of two <i>s is usually avoided. This is so in *babyish, essayist, lobbyist, rowdyism, toryism*. Word-final <-i> is rare: *ski, taxi*. For these we find *skiing*, and either *taxiing* or *taxying, taxis* or *taxies*, but for obvious reasons *<skying> is ruled out.

Rule (2) is an example of an ADAPTATION RULE which alters the spelling of a morpheme when it becomes part of a complex word. Other such rules are:

Adaptation rules

- '*full* is spelt <-ful> as a suffix, as in *fretful, spoonful*.'
- '*all* is spelt <al-> as a prefix, as in *always, altogether*.'
- 'One letter of a complex spelling is elided when the same letter follows at a morpheme boundary', giving *threshold* not <-shh->, *eighth* not <-tth>. You may not notice this in words like *fully*, which looks like <full>+<-y> (cf. *smelly*) rather than the adverbial <full>+<-ly>.

'SYLLABIFICA-TION' RULES

Most printed text is 'justified': all the lines on a page, or in a column, end in exactly the same place. The edge of the print presents a straight vertical line. Justifying is done wherever possible by juggling with slightly wider or slightly smaller spaces at the word boundaries, so that the line of print expands or contracts to end with a complete word. Sometimes this cannot be done neatly and a word has to be split over two lines, using a hyphen. The wider the page or column, the less need there will be for word division, so the best place to study this practice under pressure is in text with a narrow-column layout, as in newspapers.

EXERCISE ✎

11.2 Suppose you were printing a text and your line of type could not take a whole word at the end. Where would you split the word in the following cases?

accepted	athlete	baker	bundle	danger
defensive	dictation	eventually	festive	frisky
knickers	lastly	latest	laundry	mangey
newspaper	notable	planting	problem	product
quarter	rational	saleable	shredded	singeing
solid	spaghetti	stadium	veteran	whitish

Discussion

You will aim to leave at the end of the line part of a word that is pronounceable as one or more syllables, hence the guidelines followed by typesetters are sometimes called 'syllabification' rules. Though you will often find inconsistencies, the usual practice seems to be as follows.

(a) A single consonant letter after a short vowel usually goes before the break, as in <sol-id>,<vet-eran>, and after the break if the vowel is long: <sta-dium>, <no-table>.

(b) Whenever possible, consonant letter clusters are split evenly: <ac-cepted>, <defen-sive>, <fes-tive>, <prob-lem>, <quar-ter>, including doublets such as <brag-ged>, even though the <-gg-> stands for only one phoneme /g/.

(c) Complex letter correspondences such as <ch>, <sh>, <th>, <ck>, <gh>, other than doublets, need to be kept intact: <ath-lete>, <knick-ers>, <spa-ghetti>. This includes letters that mark a particular pronunciation: <singe-ing> (not *<sing-eing>); <dicta-tion> (not *<dictat-ion>); <ra-tional> (not *<rat-ional>); <sale-able> (not *<sal-eable>).

(d) With an odd number of consonant letters, the heavier cluster usually follows the split, as in <laun-dry>. Sometimes this gives unusual clusters, such as an initial <dl> in <bun-dle>.

(e) In a complex word, it is easier for the reader if the break occurs at an element boundary, especially a free-form boundary, as in <news-paper>, <defens-ive>, and even <pro-duct> rather than <prod-uct>. The inflectional endings <-ed>, <-er>, <-es>, <-est>, <-ing> and the ending <-ish> do not usually attract a previous consonant letter. This may override criterion (a), giving <whit-ish>, <bak-er>, <lat-est> and <leav-er> (as against <bea-ver>), but may not operate in names: <mill-er>, <Mil-ler>. Breaks such as <not-ed>, <even-tually> and <plan-ting> may mislead readers by suggesting *not*, *even* and *plan*.

(f) A general principle of balance requires both parts of the divided word to be more than one letter long. Do not split after or before a single letter (*<a-sparagus>, *<buffal-o>). This applies even when the single letter may be an element (*<frisk-y>, *<impediment-a>). There may be some temptation not to observe this in cases such as <mange-y>, where <mang-ey> would shift the <e> marker of <ge> ≡ /ʤ/. On the other hand, splits such as <dang-er>, <ranging> are quite usual.

The spelling mistakes that people make are worth a careful analysis if the teaching of literacy is to be improved. They are certainly of prime interest to spelling reformers, who look to a spelling system that would cut mistakes to a minimum. Spelling errors have social penalties. If you cannot spell you are thought to be uneducated and, by a further savage twist, unintelligent.

TYPES OF SPELLING ERROR

There is no generally used set of categories for describing spelling mistakes. For instance, if you want to help typists by devising a computer program to spot spelling errors in typing, then simple graphotactic categories due to faulty fingering, such as inversion, doubling, omission, will allow most wrong spellings to be picked out. Research into literacy problems obviously needs a wider set of categories.

A very basic difference is that between a COMPETENCE ERROR, which is a fairly consistent mis-spelling, and a PERFORMANCE ERROR, which is a temporary lapse. These can only be differentiated if you are familiar with someone's work over a period of time.

Competence errors
Performance errors

Most casual errors are simply an error of choice among competing spellings of the phoneme. So, *<compleat> is immediately recognisable as *complete* and *<prefurred> as *preferred*. The correspondence is wrong, but the phoneme can be spelt like that elsewhere. These may be called VARIANT ERRORS.

Variant errors
Slips

Other performance errors can be referred to as SLIPS. These are simply carelessness, not errors of understanding. A common type of slip is when the writer anticipates in the string of letters a later spelling that requires some attention. Doubling of the wrong letter is a very common slip: *<innacuracy> *inaccuracy*, *<ommitted> *omitted*, particularly where there are treacherous analogies such as *innocent*, *committed*. These seem to be more common when a doubled letter follows later in the word; this would account for *<ussually> *usually*. <C>-doubling seems to be a memorable graphic feature, but the location of the doubling proves less certain. Similar instances of uncertainty about the placement of a graphic feature are *<whispher> *whisper*, *<realeased> *released*, *<lenght> *length*. In these examples the letters in error are a well-formed string such as <ea>, <ph>, <kh>, <th>. An example of later misplacing, rather than anticipation, is the newspaper headline: 'PM dampens hopes of *kakhi election.' Slips in typing are more complex, because we need to discount mere off-target fingering on the keyboard: *<holixay> for *holiday*.

Analogy errors

Errors which involve confusion between elements of word structure often appear to be ANALOGY ERRORS. For instance, *<apostrophy> for *apostrophe* may be a false analogy with *atrophy*, *trophy*, instead of *catastrophe*. Uncertainty about word structure can result

Jumbling

in JUMBLING: 'They were *unindated with replies' (for *inundated*). This may be just a letter metathesis, but it might possibly represent a pronunciation.

Splits

Mistakenly putting a space boundary in what should be written as a single word can be called a SPLIT: *<to gether>, *<out side>, *<be fore>, *<in tact>. Occasionally the opposite mistake is made as a

Mergers

MERGER: 'He went on leave for *awhile.' Very subtle differences of stress and phrase structure underlie: *We went on to a night club* and *We went onto a yacht*; *We drove in to the centre* and *We drove into the hedge*; *I don't want any more jam* and *She doesn't go there anymore*. The writing system has sometimes been inconsistent. Until quite recently the one-word spelling *<alright> rather than *all right* was frowned upon, in spite of the similar forms *already*, *always*, *altogether*. It does seem necessary to distinguish the different meanings of *I found them alright* (meaning 'certainly') and *I found them all right* (meaning 'all correct'). Cf. *I have got them already* and *I have got them all ready*.

EXERCISE ✎

11.3 How would you characterise the following mistakes in written English, disregarding any possible pronunciation?

(a) Approaching the volcano, they could see the creator still smoking.
(b) He wanted to marry a devoiced woman.
(c) Cuts and liaisons should be covered by a clean plaster.
(d) Teaching was not her meteor.
(e) He handed over the reigns of his business empire to his son.

When such errors occur with adults, it may reflect a real confusion over relatively unfamiliar words. When confusion occurs as a child's spelling error, it may simply be a chance confusion of shape, an unthinking visual mix-up between words which the child knows very well. This would presumably be the case with children's errors such as *<changed> for *chased*, *<frighting> for *fighting*.

It is worth distinguishing phonetic near-misses like these from instances where the two words are pure homophones in the speaker's accent and the difference is accordingly a simple correspondence error: 'his *unwaivering support', 'the *course fishing season', or

'The soft *palette is lowered in nasal consonants.' These, too, are spellings of a different word.

Homophonous word elements, such as an affix or stem, rather than the whole word may be mistaken. A surprisingly frequent error is: 'the *proceeding letter' instead of *preceding*. These are presumably people for whom *proceed* and *precede* are homophones /prə'siːd/, rather than differing by /prə-/ – /prɪ-/.

EXERCISES ✎

11.4 What are the probable reasons for the following group of spelling mistakes?

*\<anenome\> anemone	*\<bankrupcy\> bankruptcy
*\<boundry\> boundary	*\<distingtion\> distinction
*\<emnity\> enmity	*\<goverment\> government
*\<litrature\> literature	*\<pome\> poem
*\<pumkin\> pumpkin	*\<reconise\> recognise
*\<strick\> strict	*\<vacume\> vacuum

11.5 Here is a mixed bag of spelling mistakes. What insight is necessary to avoid the errors made in the following words (the correct spelling is given in parentheses)?

(a) *\<abberrant\> (aberrant) (b) *\<baronness\> (baroness)
(c) *\<begruge\> (begrudge) (d) *\<chapple\> (chapel)
(e) *\<comming\> (coming) (f) *\<deadden\> (deaden)
(g) *\<gest\> (guest) (h) *\<grammer\> (grammar)
(i) *\<hateing\> (hating) (j) *\<histery\> (history)
(k) *\<induldge\> (indulge) (l) *\<jumpt\> (jumped)
(m) *\<maintainance\> (maintenance)
(n) *\<medisine\> (medicine) (o) *\<prefered\> (preferred)
(p) *\<ritch\> (rich) (q) *\<sine\> (sign)
(r) *\<wunder\> (wonder)

SUMMARY

- Spelling mistakes need analysis, since they represent a failure in literacy teaching.
- Mistakes can be classified into competence or performance errors, variant errors, analogy errors, jumblings, splits, mergers, lexical errors and interference errors.
- Some mistakes cannot be 'explained' by any such category other than the complexity of the present conventions.

12 MORE THAN LETTERS

> Spelling is more than just stringing letters together into words, since hyphens, apostrophes and even the spaces between words have an important role to play.

The space at the beginning and end of a written word, or a punctuation mark, defines what the writing system considers to be a 'word'. We are so accustomed to this use of spaces that it is difficult to imagine that spacing and other punctuation devices were a relatively late improvement to alphabetic writing systems. We can soon see how important spacing is by trying to read a passage without spaces, or capitals, or word-internal hyphens and without the convention of beginning a new line of text with a new word.

EXERCISES ✎

12.1 The following slab of text has been stripped of everything except the actual letters. Write it out as it would normally appear on a printed page.

> asevendonaldduckcanseethemai
> nproblemwithasimpleswitchisthati
> tsanallornoneoronoroffdevicewhyb
> othertounderstanditslimitations

Discussion

We soon see that spaces are needed to mark word boundaries. Does the text begin with *a seven* or *as even*? The string of letters <understand> has to be a single word, not a word *under* followed by a word *stand*, whereas <seethe> is not *seethe* but *see the*.

The main use of hyphens is to help to distinguish COMPOUNDS from PHRASES. This is frequently done, however, without a hyphen, using a space. The phrases *green house* and *black board* are distinguished by spacing from the compounds *greenhouse* (conservatory) and *blackboard*. Compounds have a specialised meaning, often described as 'close connection' between the elements: they are firmly stuck together. Phrases are open to expansion by inserting other words: *a green and yellow house, a green private house, a very green house.*

Compounds
Phrases

The use of hyphens is very variable, especially in noun + noun compounds. Well-used compound nouns are usually written as one word: *lamplight, lamppost, lampshade,* but they may have a hyphen as *lamp-light, lamp-post, lamp-shade.* On the whole, AmE makes less use of hyphenation than BrE.

The use of a hyphen is to some extent influenced by the stress pattern. Though compounds tend to have stress on the first element, there are many which do not. Those which, like phrases, have stress on the second element are usually written as two words: *kitchen sink, town centre, district nurse.* This is so for compounds such as *baby boy, city state, clock radio,* where a 'both ... and' relationship holds ('both a clock and a radio'). In some such compounds: *fighter-bomber, fridge-freezer, hunter-gatherer, washer-drier,* the hyphen is necessary to show that the two parts are alternatives. A *player-manager* can act as a player or as a manager or as both.

The hyphen comes into its own in various kinds of complex modifiers, as in *an on-or-off device.* Other examples are *a blue-grey tinge, forty-five degrees, large-scale efforts, parish-pump politics, I'll talk to him man-to-man.*

Prefixes ending in a vowel often have a hyphen when attached to a stem beginning with a vowel, as in *re-enact, co-exist, de-escalate.* Unhyphenated examples are more common: as in *react, reinstate, coaxial.* Unusual uses of a suffix can also be indicated by using a hyphen, as in: <a Wilde-ism>.

A common mistake in spelling is to write <it's>, as in 'on *it's own', for the possessive pronoun <its>. This wrong use of <it's> is a natural enough mistake to make, since here the two main uses of the apostrophe are in conflict with each other. The most common use of the apostrophe is to show that the possessive *Mark's* or *mark's* is different from the simple name *Marks* and noun plural *marks.* In reply to the question *What wakes you up so early?* someone may say /ðə ˈbɜː(r)dz ˈtwɪtə(r)/. This can have three different structures, since *twitter* can be either a verb or a noun. The different structures are 'the birds habitually twitter' or 'the twitter of a bird' or 'the twitter of several birds'. The three are distinguished in writing as <birds>, <bird's> and <birds'>.

There is a complication, though. Some pronouns have possessive forms ending in <s> but without any apostrophe: *hers, his, ours, theirs, yours.* This is one of several differences between the spelling of grammatical words and lexical words. So as a possessive pronoun, the spelling <its> is regular. But the misuse of *<it's> is much more extensive than mis-spellings such as *<their's>, *<your's>. That is because of confusion with the other main use of the apostrophe.

The apostrophe also serves to indicate a pronunciation in which sounds (and letters) are missing. So <it's> represents *it is* in <it's going> or *it has* in <it's gone>. This use of the apostrophe is particularly common with *not* and auxiliary verbs, such as *can't*, *don't*, *shouldn't*, *I'll*, *we'll*, *they've*, *you've*, *I'd*, *she'd*. Since these reduced forms represent colloquial speech, they are rather frowned upon in formal prose. Such an apostrophe is dropped when the shortened noun form overtakes the full form in common use. So *bus*, *cello*, *flu* and *phone*, which are shortenings of *omnibus*, *violoncello*, *influenza* and *telephone* do not now have apostrophes to cover the missing part, as <'phone>, etc.

Formerly, apostrophes were used to make plurals for abstract symbols which have names but no phonetic value: <three 7's in a row>, <mind your P's and Q's>, <the regiment has three VC's>. Present practice is to do without them too, as <7s>, <Ps and Qs> and <VCs>.

The complex of information coded by the apostrophe – whether a letter is missing, or whether a noun is possessive or just plural, or whether it is both possessive and plural – has made spellers feel insecure about its use. Apostrophes are so revered as a token of educational prowess that they have become a favourite device in 'creative' spelling, especially in notices and placards: *<Parking for lorry's>; *<Property's in your area>.

A capital (upper-case) letter differs in size and usually in shape from a small (lower-case) letter (<q>, <Q>, <a>, <A>). As a punctuation device, a capital is used to mark the beginning of a sentence. Capitals also mark the names of places, products, institutions and persons *Milton Keynes*, *Guinness*, *Lord Nelson*, *Donald Duck*, or words which have a very specific reference or a technical meaning: '. . . the admission of the New Shares to the Official List by the London Stock Exchange'.

The use of a capital 'I' in English for the first-person pronoun is highly unusual. It seems to have developed as a printing device because of the lack of bulk in a single small 'i'. In many languages it is the second-person 'you' pronouns that are given a capital letter as a mark of deference. English-speakers themselves are wary of the apparent self-centredness of *I* and pupils may be advised not to use *I* too frequently because it sticks out so much on the written page.

Switching to a different font or size of type may be used to mark emphasis:

It's *his* bloody fault, not mine.

12.2   The following samples of text contain a large number of errors. Write the text out as it would normally appear on a printed page.

   (a) *Reliable Person wanted for light house keeping job. Five day's a week with week end's off.

(b) *The post man comes early on tuesday's in Summer, but the dust bin men cant always be relied-on.
(c) *The Pennine way at it's best was all together more demanding, so we we're glad when journeys end was insight.

SUMMARY

- Spaces between words, hyphens, apostrophes and capital letters all play an essential role in the structure of written text.

UNIVERSITY COLLEGE WINCHESTER
LIBRARY

13 AMERICAN AND BRITISH SPELLING

> 'The minds of the people are in a ferment, and consequently disposed to receive improvements' (Noah Webster writing to Benjamin Franklin in 1786). Webster set out to give Americans some improved spelling conventions.

In 1783 Noah Webster (1758–1843) published his *American Spelling Book*, which sold millions of copies over the next century and a half, and in 1828 he published the first of the standard dictionaries that still bear his name.

In his *Dictionary* and *Spelling Book* he introduced changes which he felt would not be too controversial and which the public of the United States would take to. Some of his changes, such as <-ic> instead of former <-ick> in *heroic*, *public*, etc., have also been adopted independently in BrE spelling.

EXERCISE ✎

13.1 Here are some nouns which end in <-or> in AmE spelling. The spelling of some of these nouns was changed from BrE <-our> to the present AmE <-or> by Noah Webster. Which of them have the BrE <-our> ending? What common characteristic is shared by this group of nouns with BrE <-our>? Are there any exceptions?

armor	author	behavior	collector	color
error	favor	glamor	harbor	honor
humor	labor	languor	odor	pallor
parlor	rigor	rumor	splendor	squalor
stupor	terror	tumor	vapor	vigor

The ending <-re> in words such as *centre, fibre, goitre, mitre, sombre, spectre, theatre,* became AmE <-er> (*center, fiber,* etc.). Exceptions are *acre, lucre,* since *<acer>, *<lucer> would have a <c> ≡ /s/ correspondence. The older <-re> spelling does, however, have a useful marking function: it marks such nouns as different from agent nouns in <-er>. There is a contrast in BrE spelling between *metre* 'unit of length' and *meter* 'instrument'.

In the suffix <-ise>/<-ize> as in *capitalise, dramatise, naturalise,* where BrE practice varies, AmE spelling has a standard <-ize> (p. 45). In BrE *analyse* and *paralyse* require <s> spellings, but AmE is more likely to have <z>.

The unstressed prefix <en-> ≡ /ɪn/ in the BrE spelling of some words has a corresponding AmE spelling <in->: *encase, enclose, endorse, enquire, ensure,* giving *incase, inclose,* etc. This does not apply to all <en-> words: *encamp, enchant, endow,* etc. (p. 46).

The BrE <c> spelling of the nouns *defence, licence, offence, pretence* has an <s> counterpart in AmE spelling: *defense, license,* etc. AmE spells *practice* with <c> in both noun and verb; BrE distinguishes between a noun spelling (*licence, practice*) and a verb spelling (*license, practise*).

Superfluous letters have been cut in AmE spelling in several cases. The BrE digraph spellings <ae> and <oe> for /iː/ in Greek and Latin loan-words have been reduced to simple <e> in AmE spelling: *anaemia, anaesthetic, diarrhoea, encyclopaedia, foetus, mediaeval, oestrogen, paediatrics,* giving *anemia, fetus, medieval,* etc. The <e> spelling is now widely adopted in BrE. The ending <-ogue> in *analogue, catalogue, dialogue, epilogue, monologue, travelogue,* has been simplified to <-og>, giving *analog, catalog,* etc., and there is a similar reduction in *abridgement, acknowledgement,* etc., giving *abridgment,* etc.

There are differences in <C>-doubling. The single <l> at the end of BrE *appal, enthral, instil, fulfil,* is doubled in AmE spelling to give *appall,* etc. On the other hand the double <CC> in the unstressed syllables of BrE *counsellor, kidnapper, traveller, worshipping,* is usually single in AmE spelling: *counselor, kidnaper, traveler, worshiping.*

EXERCISE ✎

13.2 There are a number of BrE/AmE spelling differences in individual words. What is the usual, and in some cases obsolescent, BrE spelling of the words given here in AmE form?

artifact	carcass	jail	judgment	maneuver
mold	molt	mustache	pajamas	plow
smolder	sulfur	tire	wagon	woolen

In American popular newspaper headlines and in advertising, there is widespread creative respelling similar to that used in invented trade names. Common words often respelt include *buy* as

*<bi>, *Christmas* as *<Xmas>, *cool* as *<kool>, *crossing* as *<Xing>, *doughnut* as *<donut>, *high* as *<hi>, *low* as *<lo>, *night* as *<nite>, *please* as *<pleez>, *quick* as *<kwik>, *right* as *<rite>, *you* as *<U> and even go so far as to lose the word structure in *socks* as *<sox>, and *thanks* as *<thanx>. The shortened forms <tho> for *though*, <thru> for *through* have become well established in AmE.

There are some differently spelt pairs of words in BrE spelling that reduce to a single spelling in AmE: *cheque* → *check*, *draught* → *draft*, *kerb* → *curb*, *storey* → *story*.

SUMMARY

- Noah Webster was mainly responsible for the present differences between AmE and BrE spelling through the prestige of his *Dictionary* and his popular *Spelling Book*.

SPELLING REFORM

14

> Traditional English spelling has evolved over many centuries, absorbing wave after wave of foreign loan-words. Is it now time to tidy up some of the anomalies to give greater consistency to the whole system?

If English spelling could be made more regular

- it would be easier and quicker for children to learn to read and write;
- foreign learners of English would find in the spelling a clearer indication of the pronunciation;
- less complex spellings, such as *<tho> for *though*, would save effort, time, ink and paper.

People readily accept these reasons, but it is difficult to find political support for actually implementing them. Here are short specimens of two very different proposals that have been designed to reform traditional English spelling.

EXERCISES ✎

14.1 What kinds of change are suggested in the following sample text? It may help you to know that the scheme is called *Cut Spelling* (CS).

> Th reduced space requiremnt has typograficl benefits; public syns and notices cud be smalr, or ritn larjr; mor text cud be fitd on video or computer screens; fewr abreviations wud be needd and fewr words wud hav to be split with hyfns at th ends of lines. ... Less imediatly obvius is the fact that CS removes many of th most

trublsm spelng problms that hav bedevld riting in english for centuris.

Discussion

Most schemes for spelling reform get rid of letters that are not relevant to the pronunciation. CS makes this its basic principle. The above sample of CS is taken from one of the Simplified Spelling Society's promotional leaflets. A reform of this type was suggested by an Australian psychologist, Valerie Yule, in the 1970s. Text in which surplus and misleading letters were dropped from the spelling speeded up adult reading and seemed to help backward readers make fewer mistakes. Detailed proposals for CS have since been published in Britain by a working group of the Simplified Spelling Society (p. 95).

Earlier reformers had to some extent tried to get rid of redundant letters. Noah Webster, responsible for most of the present differences in spelling between AmE and BrE conventions (pp. 64–6), would have liked to go even further than his publishers allowed in cutting out superfluous letters. He had hoped to get rid of final <-e> in words such as *<gazell>, *<definit>, *<disciplin>, *<doctrin>, *<granit>, *<imagin>, *<maiz>, *<nightmar>, *<vultur>. Dropping other superfluous letters would still leave the following recognisable: *<chesnut>, *<crum>, *<diaphram>, *<grotesk>, *<ile>, *<ismus>, *<mosk>, *<thum>. In many words vowel digraphs could be simplified: *<bredth>, *<fether>, *<lepard>, *<stelth>, *<thred>, *<juce>, *<nusance>. However, it was thought that public opinion would not tolerate these further changes to AmE spelling.

Apart from general economy of writing effort and the cost of printing, there are some distinct advantages in getting rid of redundant letters. If *organ* is spelt *<orgn>, *stationary* and *stationery* as *<stationry>, *principal* and *principle* as *<principl>, there is no longer any problem for the writer in how to represent the vowel of the unstressed syllable. Most letters representing /ə/ before <l, m, n, r> are cut out and most doubled <C>-letters are made single. So, *add* can become *<ad> and *added* then becomes *<add>.

Most CS alterations are made by cutting what is there in the traditional spelling. With a loss of <a> in *peace* and <i> in *piece*, both become *<pece>. On the other hand, the spelling of *vane, vain, vein*, remains unchanged. The <e> of *computer* is kept, because it marks the previous vowel as long, but the <e> of *fewer* is cut to give *<fewr>.

CS does not seek to alter correspondences where there are no redundant letters. It does, however, have three substitution rules: replacing <igh> with <y> as a spelling of /aɪ/ (*<fytng> *fighting*), and has <j> as a consistent spelling of /dʒ/ (*<brij> *bridge*) and <f> for /f/ (*<fotografd>, *<enuf>). The {-ed} suffix is cut to {-d}, to give *<ripd>, *<relentd>, *<begd>, etc. Phoneme clusters such as */pd/, */td/, */kd/ are not found in English. You can have voiceless clusters /pt/, /kt/, as in *apt, act* or voiced clusters /bd/, /gd/, as in *robbed, begged*, but you cannot mix voiced and voiceless consonants. This makes it possible to use contrasting spellings *<rapt>, *<rapd>, for *rapt*, *rapped*, since there is otherwise no form ending in *<-pd>.

Occasional homographs, such as *<latrly> for *latterly* and *laterally*, are not thought to be serious. On the other hand groups of spellings which would become ambiguous by cutting are preserved: *binned, chilled, finned, grinned, milled, willed* retain their letter doubling as *<binnd> etc. to avoid confusion with *bind, child, grind, mild*, etc. *Thumb, bomb, lamb, plumb*, have their <b> cut to give *<thum>, etc., but *climb, comb, tomb, womb* keep their <b>, somewhat oddly, as a marker of the long vowel.

Cutting often applies to the vowel letters of unstressed syllables. *Operate* becomes *<oprate> and *military* *<militry>. It may prove difficult for the reader to cope with resulting compressed strings of consonant letters, such as the *<-rwrdl-> of *<forwrdly>, or *<implmntng> for *implementing*.

The overall saving in written letters seems to be about 10 per cent. This is, naturally enough, thought to be worthwhile. However, the basic assumption of 'economy' needs to be tested and explored. One of the striking features of human language is its high redundancy, which allows it to operate in adverse conditions. Not every part of a written or spoken message needs to be consciously monitored by the listener or reader. But if CS takes out some of the slack in the system, then more attention and conscious effort may be required as a result. How is that to be costed?

It is tempting to cut out the <o> in the adjectival ending <-ous> to give *<piteus>, *< hideus>, *< famus>, *< rigrus>, but that gets rid of a marker which separates the <-ous> of adjectives from the <-us> of nouns (*radius, citrus*). It is tempting to reduce *tea, fee, key*, to *<te>, *<fe>, *<ke>, but then we have lost a marker of the difference on the printed page between stressed lexical words and unstressed function words such as *be, me, we* (p. 76).

The 'redundant' letters, naturally enough, have been identified as redundant by people who are already highly literate. They ask themselves 'Are these cuts possible for a skilled reader like me?' But a learner who is dependent on reference back to speech is not necessarily going to find *<implmntng> as easy to tackle, in either reading or writing, as <implementing>, which clearly has its four syllables marked by vowel letters. Similarly, *anatomist* spelt as *<anatmist> may be read from cold as */ˈænətmɪst/, on the lines of *columnist*. People in general have no problem at all with counting syllables. They will tell you that *implementing* has four syllables and *forwardly* has three. Faced with an unfamiliar word, they will usually find in the traditional spelling a useful syllabic framework for their attempted reading. But there is no indication in *<megloplis> for *megalopolis* that the word has more than three syllables.

An initial learner will be expected to master CS as a new and independent writing system. This is claimed to be easier than learning traditional spelling, because the text has been stripped of redundant letters and hence should have greater regularity.

14.2 Here are a few words for you to respell in the CS system by getting rid of surplus letters. Obviously you will find it difficult after only a short introduction to the scheme. The odds are that your versions will not match the proposed version very well, since you have not had time to learn the system properly. But the point of the exercise is to bring you face-to-face with the design problems.

acknowledgement	boutique	broadening	connoisseur
excelsior	flummoxed	kippers	kneaded
language	origin	phosphorus	psychology
roughage	spherical	wholesome	wriggling

14.3 What is the basic idea underlying the completely different approach shown in the following specimen? Here, too, look carefully at each respelling and ask: what do these changes achieve?

Agaen, let us not forget huu form dhe graet majorrity ov dhoez dhat lurn to reed and riet. Dhae ar dhe children dhat atend priemary skuulz; dhaer tiem iz limited. We hav noe riet to impoez on dhem a kaotik speling for dhe saek ov posibly teeching dhem a litl historrikal gramar.

(from *New Spelling*; see 'Further reading', p. 95)

Discussion

The principle of alphabetic writing in its strictest form requires only one written symbol for each phoneme and only one phoneme for each written symbol. With such a system, anyone who knows the pronunciation of a word should be able to spell it and anyone who sees the word written should be able to pronounce it. Some spelling reformers have tried to bring English spelling closer to this ideal. The most detailed approach to a consistent phonemic spelling has been 'New Spelling' (NS). It uses single-letter spellings eked out with digraphs, while preserving the present spelling of some unstressed endings.

Most of the changes affect vowel spellings. The moving of the <e> marker for long vowels *<graet>, *<tiem>, *<theem>, *<impoez>, *<fued> for *great, time, theme, impose, feud* is not very startling, since such digraphs are familiar anyway from words such as *lie, toe, cue*. Simple /uː/ without /j/ is <uu>, giving *food, feud* as *<fuud>, *<fued>. The <oo> spelling is used for short /ʊ/, with *good, put, could* as *<good>, *<poot>, *<cood>.

The most striking change in the original NS proposals was the visual shock of separating the spelling of /θ/ with <th> and /ð/ with <dh>. It has since been suggested that the *<dh> should be dropped in favour of retaining <th> for both phonemes (see pp. 28, 79 to appreciate why this is feasible).

The {ed} of *hoped, rushed, begged, skimmed, played, emptied* has a phonemic spelling as *<hoept>, *<rusht>, *<begd>, *<skimd>, *<plaed>, *<emptid>, so *tacked* and *tact, allowed* and *aloud*, are not distinguished: they are spelt *<takt>, *<aloud>. On the other hand, there is no attempt to represent vowel reduction to /ə/ in unstressed affixes with a common single letter. Endings such as <-ant> and <-ent> are kept intact because of the accented vowel in derived forms, as in *pedant – *pedantik, *prezident – *prezidenshl.

Consonants required little alteration: <g> is reserved for /g/, so /ʤ/ is spelt with <j>: rage as *<raej>. The letter <k> was chosen for /k/, largely because of its more distinctive shape. The spellings <c>, <ck>, <q> and <x> were no longer needed. The digraph <ch>, however, is required for /ʧ/, since church (unchanged) is clearly preferable to *<tshurtsh> and <ch> replaces <tch> in *<pich>. The <h> of <ch> is in fact redundant and there were tentative plans to drop it at a later stage, which would leave *<curc> for church. With single <c> gone, <s> and <z> were consistently used for /s/ and /z/. Phonemic consistency also meant that if <ng> were kept for /ŋ/, then /ŋg/ would have to be represented as <ngg>, giving longer as *<longger>. The phoneme /ʒ/ is spelt as <zh>, giving leisure, usual as *<lezher>, *<uezhueal>.

Double <C>-letters are not used in NS to mark short vowels since vowel digraphs with <e> are used to show vowel length consistently: doll, dole became *<dol>, *<doel>. Double-consonant phonemes at word boundaries are naturally spelt double (meanness as *<meennes>) and <-orr-> is given a double <-rr-> in *<forren>, *<majorrity>, to avoid confusion with <or> ≡ /ɔː(r)/.

Here are a few names respelt in NS. These bring home one of the disadvantages of such a radical change. It causes a great deal of visual disruption.

*<Inggland> *England* *<Jurmany> *Germany*
*<Uerugwie> *Uruguay* *<Uerop> *Europe*
*<Aesha> *Asia* *<Juulyus Seezar> *Julius Caesar*
*<Vurjil> *Vergil* *<Konfueshyus> *Confucius*

14.4 Spell the word list (*boutique*, etc.) given in Exercise 14.2 in NS. Here, too, the important thing is to try to follow the conventions for yourself.

New Spelling and *Cut Spelling* are both very radical approaches to spelling reform. There is, however, a third informal alternative: to expand the regularities of the present system. A softly-softly staged reform could be made by publishing lists of recommended respellings of irregularly spelt words. The difficulty is to know when to stop. The <igh> spelling of /aɪ/ has the merit of being unambiguous for the reader, but it would help the writer if it were changed to a more regular <i ... e> to give *<lite>, *<brite>, *<briten>, *<delite>, *<tite>, *<sie>, etc. The notion of regularity to be aimed at would be found within the present system. Similarly, we might have *<ruff>, *<tuff>, *<troff>, *<coff>, for <-ough> spellings.

Sooner or later even softly-softly reformers would have to tackle the present untidy marking of vowel length. Do we keep <C>-doubling as a marker of short vowels and extend it to give *<chappel>, *<lemmon>, *<devvil>? Do we keep different spellings for homophones such as *vane*, *vain*, *vein*, or can we have *<vane> for all three? Do we keep final <-e> as a marker of long vowels but put it next to the previous vowel letter, as in *<daenger>, *<deemon>, *<pielot>, *<roebust>, *<trueth>? Should BrE practice follow AmE and reverse the <-re> of *centre* to give *<center>, *<fiber>, *<somber>, *<theater>? Do we also make a similar switch with *apple* to get *<appel>, *<bottel>, *<cattel>, *<trubbel>?

Proposals for the reform of English spelling are not far to seek. Whether reforms can ever be made is a political question.

EXERCISE ✎

14.5 Suggest a list of relatively irregular spellings that you would like to see reformed in a way that people might accept as reasonable. Compare your choice of words and your suggested respellings with those of other people. Be aware of the wider consequences of changes you would like to see.

SUMMARY

- There is no fundamental reason why English spelling cannot be reformed, just as the centuries-old British £ s d currency system was decimalised in the early 1970s.
- Lists of irregular words suited for respelling in a more regular form may be able to attract a measure of political support, given the increasing concern about standards of literacy. More radical schemes for a comprehensive spelling reform have failed so far to muster political will.

ANSWERS TO EXERCISES

1.3 There are ten words with two phonemes:

ache, ape, buy, dough, ease, eight, inn, ought, two, who; sixteen words with three phonemes: *bath, bathe, blue, choice, choose, cough, debt, eggs, half, one, patch, plough, right, through, write, youth;* nine words with four phonemes: *bring, shred, since, stray, tax, think, thread, twine, wrench.*

2.1 The missing words are:

(1e) leper, (1h) leap, (2b) bail/bale, (3b) tail/tale, (4a) debt, (4d) die/dye, (4g) bud, (5c) duck, (5f) reek, (5h) leek/leak, (6d) guy, (6h) league, (7f) reach, (8b) jail/gaol, (8e) ledger, (8g) budge, (9a) met, (9c) dumb, (9f) ream, (10c) done/dun, (10d) nigh, (10h) lean, (11g) bung, (12b) fail, (13b) veil/vale, (13c) dove, (13h) leave, (14f) wreath, (15f) wreathe, (16d) sigh, (17g) buzz, (18d) shy, (20d) high, (21c) dull, (22b) rail, (23d) why, (24a) yet.

2.2 The missing words are:

(1a) pin, (1f) kin, (2d) fell, (3a) pan, (3f) can, (4c) stood, (5b) hut, (5e) luck, (6f) con.

2.3 The missing words are:

(8b) key/quay, (8d) feel, (8e) leak/leek, (9a) bay, (9c) staid/stayed, (9d) fail, (9f) cane, (10a) by/bye/buy, (10e) like, (11b) coy, (11f) coin, (12d) fool, (13f) cone, (14d) foul/fowl.

2.5   The words in phonemic transcription are:

quick, service, youth, chairs, join, harsh, thought, treasure, idea, hunger, those, shank.

UNIT 3
Long and short vowel pairs

3.1   Suitable words for completing the word pairs include:

- /eɪ/–/æ/: grateful, hilarity, humane, manic, opaque, static, pallid/pallor, sane, shadow, tenacity, vale; Spaniard, vanity;
- /iː/–/e/: austerity, credence, feminine, helical, heroine, legal, obscenity, severity, supremacy; bereft, cleanse, health, heath, settle, shepherd;
- /aɪ/–/ɪ/: bible, crime, define, fifty/fifth, linear, lyre, mimic, mine, reconciliation, reside, satirical, type;
- /oʊ/–/ɒ/: atrocious, close, colliery, florid, holiday, ominous, provocative, sole, tone;
- /aʊ/–/ʌ/: renunciation, Southern.

UNIT 4
Marking vowel length

4.1   The consonant letter is simply repeated to provide <C>-doubling in twelve of the twenty-four consonants, as in:

su**pp**er	ri**bb**on	mu**tt**er	we**dd**ing	da**gg**er	o**ff**er
bo**ss**y	di**zz**y	fo**ll**ow	mi**rr**or	su**mm**er	fu**nn**y

One other consonant, /v/, may very occasionally have <C>-doubling. This only occurs in some slang words such as *luvvies*, *flivver*, *navvy*, *bovver*, *revving*. There is no <-vv-> doubling in ordinary words such as *devil*, *grovel*, *living*, *seven*. This restriction on the use of <-vv-> seems to follow from the development of <w> as an individual consonant letter in the Middle English period, which came to be called 'double <u>'.

4.2   The normal doubling of <k> in native words is <ck>, as in *sock*, *tick*, *bracket*, *chicken*. Compare *stoking – stocking*, *baker – backer*.

The phoneme /tʃ/ (as in *hitch*, *catch*, *butcher*, *satchel*) has <ch> as its 'single' spelling and <tch> as its 'doubled' spelling; compare *beach – batch*.

The phoneme /dʒ/ (as in *bridge*, *cadge*, *gadget*, *ledger*) has <g(e)> as its 'single' spelling and <dg(e)> as its 'doubled' spelling, as in *cage – cadge*.

4.4   The final <-e> of *tile* and *tape* marks the vowel as long. In addition, the <C>-doubling of *till* positively marks the vowel there as short. The word *tap* has no such marker, but we know the vowel is short simply because it is not marked as long by a final <-e>.

Before the end of a word, <p, b, t, d, g, m, n> do not double to mark a preceding short vowel: *rip, rob, bit, mad, rag, dim, con*. This is also the case historically with <r> in *mar*. The vowel needs marking with a final <-e> to be long: *ripe, robe, bite, made, rage, dime, cone*, *mare*. When suffixes beginning with a vowel letter are added, normal doubling occurs: *shrub – shrubbery, fad – faddist, sip – sipping, ram – rammed*. This restriction on final doubling may not apply in personal names: *Bragg, Chubb, Grimm, Penn, Starr, Whipp*.

In effect final <C>-doubling is largely restricted to <ff> *stiff*, <ss> *miss*, <ll> *dull*, <ck> *pick*, <tch> *catch*, <dge> *cadge*. There is a twofold marking of vowel length in *till – tile, chaff – chafe, doss – dose, pick – pike, cadge – cage*.

In recent French loan-words, such as *charade* and *latrine*, <a> and <i> have their unshifted values /ɑː/ and /iː/, rather than /eɪ/ and /aɪ/. Exceptionally there may be no <e>-marking, as in *motif* /moʊˈtiːf/.

An important restriction on <e>-marked vowel spellings is that the marked vowel is spelt by a single vowel letter. So we do not find *<meate>, *<soake>, *<veile>, *<taile>. Usually there is a single consonant letter before the <-e>, with an occasional exception, such as <-aste> in *haste, paste, taste, waste*.

4.5 The final consonants in these words are /ð/, /s/ and /z/. The <-e> in *bathe, breathe, loathe, wreathe* marks the vowel as long and more significantly marks the consonant as /ð/ rather than the /θ/ of *bath, breath, loath, wreath*. Other examples with a marked /ð/ are *lathe, lithe, swathe*. In *mouth* (verb) and *smooth* the /ð/ is not marked.

The function of <-e> in the other words is best seen in *browse, copse, lapse, please, tease, tense*. It prevents the final <s> being confused with the plural morpheme of *brows, cops, laps, pleas, teas, tens*. Its function in the whole group of words is to mark them as single morphemes. As such it is called 'lexical <-e>'.

4.6

agreeing	bathing	blueish	browsing	cadging
canoeing	changing	elopement	fatiguing	festivity
finely	gaugeable	glueing	hateful	hinging
judg(e)ment	likeable	loathing	loving	management
mated	mating	mileage	modish	moving
noticeable	palish	paleness	plaguing	rescuing
saleable	singeing	teasing	traceable	valuing

Not without reason, spellers are often very uncertain about when to delete the final <-e> of a word if an ending is added. In some words practice varies. BrE generally has *acknowledgement, abridgement* and *judgement*, but AmE generally has *acknowledgment, abridgment, judgment*. The <e> is not needed since the spelling <-dgm-> can only represent /-dʒm-/. The <dgm> spelling is gaining ground in BrE. It has a long-established use as the *judgment* of a court. An English judge might well write 'in giving my judgment in this case, I shall use my judgement in assessing . . .'

The basic rule is simple enough: the <-e> is deleted if the ending begins with a vowel, giving *fatiguing, festivity, loving, modish*, *movable, palish, plaguing.* Before a consonant there is no deletion: *hateful, finely, elopement, paleness.*

The <e> that marks long vowels, as in *mate*, is regularly deleted before the inflections {-ed}, {-ing}, as in *mated, mating*. This is no confusion since <C>-doubling takes over the task of marking the vowel length: *mate* and *mat* become *mated, matted,* and *mating, matting*. The <e> that follows a stem-final /z/, /ð/ or /v/ is also deleted: *browsing, easing, loathing, loving, festivity*. This makes {bathe} and {bath} homographs in *bathing, bathed*.

The <-e> is usually kept when it is a marker of the pronunciation of the previous consonant such as the /dʒ/ in *gaugeable, manageable,* and the /s/ in *noticeable, traceable*. A spelling *<noticable> would invite <c> ≡ /k/ before the <a> as in *practicable* /'præktɪkəbl/. So, *singeing* with /ndʒ/ is kept different from *singing* with /ŋ/. But this is only done when you know that there is such a pair to keep distinct. Since there are no words */'ʧæŋɪŋ/ or */'hɪŋɪŋ/, the <-e> is dropped in *changing, hinging,* from *change, hinge*. Dictionary makers allow some undeleted forms before <-able> such as *likeable, saleable*.

The <e> in the vowel digraphs <-ee> and <-oe> is not deleted before <-i->, giving *agreeing, seeing, canoeing, shoeing, toeing*, etc. The reason is no doubt that the loss of <e> would cause confusion between <ei> and <oi> if we had *<seing>, *<shoing>. The <e> of the digraph <-ue> is usually deleted, as in *arguing, barbecuing, continuing, pursuing, queuing, rescuing, subduing, valuing,* and in *truism*. On the other hand, there is free variation between *blueish, bluish, cueing, cuing, glueing, gluing*. The spelling *blueish* preserves the written shape of the morpheme, whereas *bluish* begins to look uncomfortably like *blush*. Nor is the <-e> deleted in *bluey, gluey,* since *<bluy>, *<gluy>, begin to resemble the <uy> spelling in *buy, guy*.

UNIT 5
Complications in length marking

Short word rule

5.1 Function words (pronouns, prepositions, conjunctions, auxiliary verbs) are generally spelt with no more than two letters: *am, as, at, be, do, he, if, in, is, it, me, of, on, or, to, up, us, we,* but *she* cannot have less than three because there is no single letter to stand for /ʃ/. The lexical words, on the other hand, are usually bulked up to a minimum of three letters. This bulking up is known as the 'SHORT WORD RULE'.

Lexical monosyllables consisting of a single vowel must have both a vowel digraph and <e>-marking (*eye, owe*).

The long vowels of /CV/ lexical words must have either at least a vowel digraph or <e>-marking (*nigh, low, die, bye*). The <-e> is usually kept in the suffixed forms *ageing, ageism, ageist,* unlike the regular *raging, staging*.

Short vowels in /VC/ lexical words must be marked by unusual <C>-doubling: *add, ebb, egg, inn, odd* compared with *pad, web, beg, tin, nod*.

Function words have an unusual single <o> spelling of /u:/ in *do*, rather than *<doo>, and similarly in *to, who, two* and *thro,* the shortened form of *through*. This is avoided in *shoe*. The word *if* does not have word-final doubling, as in *cuff, stiff.*

It would seem that *ox* is an exception to the short word rule, since it is a lexical word spelt with two letters. However, *ox* could be regarded as outside the scope of the rule, since <x> is not a consonant letter that can be doubled. The word *axe* has an alternative spelling *ax*. It may well be that the spelling *axe* comes from a reanalysis of the plural *axes* as <axe>+<s> rather than <ax>+<es>. Another apparent exception is *go*. Its limited use as a borderline auxiliary verb, as in *I'm going to do it*, hardly makes it a function word. A normal spelling would be *<goe>.

Abbreviations of lexical words such as *bo* 'hobo', *ma, pa*, do not observe the short word rule, though *OED* does cite a variant *pah*, which did not catch on. The early names of some musical notes did not observe the rule: *do, re, mi, fa, so, la, ti*. Later spellings have provided alternatives to some of these: *doh, ray, fah, soh, lah*, using <h>, untypically for English, to indicate a long vowel. The word *hum*, which simply refers to the sound [m], has been bulked up with an initial <h>.

Occasional exotic <CV> words such as *ti* 'tropical plant' and *bo* 'Senegalese tree' do not seriously affect the rule. For the reader, they are clearly marked as exotic by the spelling. Science is allowed liberties such as *id*, which may be 'one of three divisions of the psyche' or 'an allergic reaction to an agent causing an infection'.

Bulking up of short lexical words associates size with stress and makes the lexical words stand out on the printed page. In the seventeenth century, *be, he, she, ye*, could be spelt both with and without an extra <-e> to show the difference between unstressed weak forms and stressed strong forms, as in John Donne's:

> For every man alone thinkes he hath got
> To be a Phoenix, and that then can bee
> None of that kinde, of which he is, but hee.
> (John Donne *An Anatomie of the World*, (1611), lines 216ff.)

where *he, be*, represent weak forms and *hee, bee*, represent stressed forms.

5.2 These words end in one of the suffixes <-ic>, <-id>, <-ule>. The <-ic> adjectives usually have a long vowel in the related base form: *athlete, cone, gene, state, tone*. In discussing the vowel shift, we saw that when a short vowel varies with a long vowel in different allomorphs (pp. 14–15), there is no <C>-doubling to mark the short vowel.

There is a small group of apparent exceptions which do have a doubled <-CC-> spelling before <-ic(al)>: *attic, ferric, metallic, phallic, prussic, tannic, traffic, tyrannical*. The stressed vowel here does not alternate with a long vowel in other forms. The nouns *traffic* and *attic* would perhaps be more consistently spelt *<traffick> and *<attick> like nouns such as *derrick* and *gimmick*.

Some nouns in <-ule> may also relate to base forms with a long vowel: *globe, grain, mode, node.*

5.3 There are two kinds of word here. The <-ish> of *reddish* is a suffix added to a free form *red* with normal <C>-doubling. The <-ish> of *radish* is not a suffix. The word is not derived from a stem *<rad>.

Minimal free forms such as *radish* do not have <C>-doubling before the <-ish>: *abolish* (not *<abollish>), and similarly *astonish, banish, blemish, cherish, finish, flourish, nourish, parish, polish, punish, radish, relish, vanish.* All these are either words in which the <-ish> is added to a bound form (*punish*; cf. *punitive*) or words which are single morphemes (*parish*). The only exception with <C>-doubling seems to be *rubbish.*

Words in which {-ish} is an adjective-forming suffix added to free forms with a short vowel will have <C>-doubling: *bullish, clannish, mannish, piggish, reddish, Scottish, skittish.*

5.4

- bridal, brutal, fatal, final, floral, frugal, global, legal, lethal, local, naval, oral, penal, regal, rival, tribal, vital, vocal;
- binary, library, notary, primary, rotary;
- cogent, decent, latent, moment, potent, prudent, recent, regent, strident, student, trident;
- apron, bison, colon, demon, ikon, mason, matron, micron, moron, nylon, patron, proton, pylon;
- favour, humour, labour, rumour, tumour, vapour (with <-or> in AmE).

5.5 Final unstressed syllables may have <C>-doubling if they have full vowel quality and hence some degree of stress. This is often the case with unstressed /æ/, as in *formatted, handicapped, kidnapped.* Some such are variable: *combatting – combating.* This does not apply to the /-ʌp/ of *hiccuped, hiccuping.*

There is normally no <C>-doubling if the last vowel in the stem is /ə/ or /ɪ/. So we have *orbited* (not *<orbitted>) and similarly:

balloted	banqueting	beckoned	bigoted
chirruped	cosseted	credited	galloped
gossiping	rocketed	vomiting	walloped

Worship is an exception: *worshipped, worshipper, worshipping.*

Words ending in the letter <c> double it to <ck> to preserve a /k/ pronunciation before <i> and <e>: *bivouacked, picnicked, trafficking.*

In BrE, but not in AmE spelling, there is usually doubling of <l> in *carolling, chancellor, channelling, counsellor, duellist, equalling, labelled, levelling, marshalled, modelling, pencilled, quarrelling, signalling, traveller,* etc. The <ll> of *skill, will,* may be kept or simplified in *skillful, skilful, willful, wilful*. This variation is not found before <-ful> preceded by <ss>: *blissful, distressful, stressful, successful*. *Gravelly* needs a double <-ll-> to distinguish it from *gravely*.

Some words ending in single <s> may or may not double it: *biassed – biased, busses – buses, bussing – busing, focussed – focused*.

The stress pattern is relevant to verbs ending in <-er>. Those with stress on the last syllable of the base form, *confer, defer, prefer, refer*, have <C>-doubling in their inflected forms *conferring, deferred, preferred, referring*, as do *disbarring, abhorring, demurring*. On the other hand, *differ, offer, proffer, suffer*, with stress on the first syllable have single <-r->, as in *differed, offering, proffered, sufferer*.

5.7 Examples of derived English words that retain the <C>-doubling of a Latinate stem are:

> {ann/enn} 'year' in *annual, annuity, centennial, perennial*;
> {bell} 'war' in *belligerent, bellicose, rebellion*;
> {fall} 'deceit' in *fallacy, fallacious, fallible*;
> {flamm}, differing from its isolate form <flame>, in *inflammable, inflammation, inflammatory*;
> {horr} 'dread' (by way of 'rough', 'bristly', 'repulsive') in *horrendous, horrible, horrific*;
> {narr} in *narrate, narrative, narration*;
> {terr} 'earth, land' in *terrestrial, territory, terrier* ('a dog which digs out hunted prey', not 'a frightful dog');
> {terr} 'fear' in *terror, terrible, terrify*.

5.8 The ending <ion> has doubled <-ll-> in *billion, bullion, million, mullion, pillion, stallion*, and *galleon* follows suit. Words longer than these usually have single <-l->: *battalion, pavilion, vermilion*. Note the irregularity with doubled and single <r> in *carrion – clarion*.

6.1 The spelling <th> may represent one of three phonemes: /θ, ð, t/. Function words such as *that, the, then, there, these, this* as a group have initial /ð/. Lexical words of native English origin have /θ/ at the beginning and end of a word, as in *bath, both, thigh, think, thread*, and they have /ð/ in the middle, as in *bother, brother, fathom, lather, wither*. By 'word' here we mean a minimal free form, to account for the /θ/ at the boundary in *earthy, healthy, frothy, ruthless, toothsome*. On the other hand, *earthen, smithy, worthy*, have /ð/ though they are not simple words. The /ð/ of *bathe, loathe, wreathe* was formerly medial before a verbal ending of which only the letter <-e> remains. Scientific and scholarly terms derived from Greek have /θ/ in all three positions: *theorem, theology, cathode, sympathy, monolith, psychopath*.

The names *Anthony, Thames, Thailand, Thomas* have /t/, as does the herb *thyme*. Some names may have /θ/: *Bertha, Kathleen, Theodore*.

**UNIT 6
Some consonant spellings**

6.2 Before <e>, <i>, <y>, the letter <g> usually spells /ʤ/, as in group (b). There are quite a few exceptions, however, including the common words *begin, get, gift, give, together.* Other exceptions include *bogy, gear, gecko, geese, gelding, gestapo, geyser, giddy, giggle, gild, gilt, gimlet, gimmick, target, yogi.*

In group (c) the words have a letter <u> as a marker of /g/. This <u> has nothing to do with the spelling of the next phoneme, it simply means 'choose /g/ here as you would before a <u>'. In *guarantee, guard*, the <u> is not really necessary; cf. *garden.* In some Latinate words, such as *distinguish, language, languid, penguin,* before an unstressed syllable <ngu> spells /ŋgw/. There is some divergence with <ng> as /nʤ/ in *ginger, danger,* and as /ŋg/ in *finger, anger.*

6.3 In teaching reading skills, some letters may be referred to as 'silent', since letters are thought to 'speak' to the reader. Letters, of course, are 'silent' in the nature of things, being graphic shapes. But we need to improve on this 'silence' imagery, because there are three fairly distinct kinds of letter function involved.

Empty letter

Letters which have no function at all, such as the <b> of *debt, doubt, dumb, lamb,* can be referred to as EMPTY. If you remove the letter <b>, there is still a viable spelling *<det>, *<lam>.

Auxiliary letter

If a letter is an essential part of a complex spelling, it is an AUXILIARY letter: <e> is part of <i ... e> in *time* , <h> is frequently used as an auxiliary letter in <sh>, <ch>, <th>, distinguishing *shave, choke, thin* from *save, coke, tin.* The <h> in *Anthony*, however, is empty. The <u> is empty in *guarantee, guard*, (see Exercise 6.2 above), but it is an auxiliary letter in the complex spelling <gu> ≡ /g/ in *guess, guide.*

Inert letter

The <g> of *sign* is different. It is INERT in *sign, signed, signing, signer*, but is active as <g> ≡ /g/ in *signal, signature, signatory.* The common morpheme in both these sets has the same written form for the reader. Similarly, if the /t/ is elided in *hasten* /ˈheɪsn/, *listen, Christmas*, the <t> is inert. Of the words with final <mb>, *bomb* has an inert <b> because of *bombard.*

The <w> of *two* is less obviously inert, but the morpheme recurs with <w> ≡ /w/ in *twain, twenty, twin, between.* Similarly the <p> in *receipt* is inert because of *receptacle, reception.*

6.4 Three phonemes, /ʧ, ʃ, k/ are here spelt as <ch>. The choice is dictated largely by a word's origin. The spelling <ch> ≡ /ʧ/ is typical of group (a) native English words and group (b) some early French loans from the medieval period that now seem equally 'basic' to ordinary spellers. Of these, the early loan *rich*, from French, and the native forms *much, such, which* stand out as irregular. After a short vowel a 'doubled' spelling <-tch> would be normal, as in *pitch, match, crutch.*

Later French loans in (c) and (d) usually reflect the modern French spelling with <ch> ≡ /ʃ/. Before final <e> we have /ʃ/, as in *niche.*

Some words may even retain a French 'accent' mark: <attaché>, <cliché>, <crèche>. Awareness of 'Frenchness' may be partly decided by other spellings in the word. If you opt for long <i ... e> ≡ /iː/ (*machine*) or <et> ≡ /eɪ/ (*sachet*), then you are in a 'French' subsystem which will further require <ch> ≡ /ʃ/.

The sound /k/ occurs in scientific and scholarly terms derived from Greek, as in groups (e) and (f). This origin, too, is difficult to make use of, since some words such as *chemist, mechanic, orchestra* are hardly specialised terms. Context restricts the choice to some extent. The clusters <chl-> and <chr-> have to be /kl-/ and /kr-/. Final <ch> ≡ /k/, as in *epoch, eunuch, monarch, stomach*, is relatively uncommon.

There are a couple of oddities here. The word *chivalry* is obviously a medieval loan and would normally have /tʃ/. The present-day /ʃ/ pronunciation comes from a desire to assert its 'Frenchness'. The verb *ache* was originally spelt <ake>, like *bake*, but Dr Samuel Johnson in his Dictionary of 1755 wrongly thought that it was Greek in origin and so spelt it <ache>.

6.5 Since <c> ≡ /s/ only occurs before <e, i, y>, there is <s> rather than <c> before any other vowel letter: *aerosol, dinosaur, persuade*. The letter <s> also occurs before a consonant, as in *scheme, slide, sphere, stay, despot, disgust, dismay*, and after a consonant in final clusters, sometimes with <e>-marking: *else, lapse*. The cluster /ns/, however, may be spelt either <-nce>, as in *advance, dance, fence, once*, or <-nse> as in *dense, rinse, sense, tense*. The <s> spelling here may have a related form in <d>: *expanse, expense, response, suspense*. See, too, p. 43.

The letter <c> does not normally occur in word-final position, so we know there is <s> at the boundary within *curiosity, jealousy*.

The endings <-cy> and <-sy> are difficult to pin down. Forms with <-sy> often relate to /t/ elsewhere: *ecstatic, heretic, epileptic, hypocrite*, but so do *secrecy* and *primacy*. *Atrocity* is likely to be confused with *animosity, generosity*. After a free form there is <-cy>: *colonelcy, normalcy*.

The stems {cede}, {ceive}, {cept}, {cess}, {cide}, {cise} and the endings <-ence>, <-ance> account for <c> ≡ /s/ in a large number of Latinate words and are best remembered as whole elements. When /s/ varies in a morpheme with /k/, as in *electric, electricity, genetic, geneticist*, the spelling is <c>.

Yet in Latinate words the ordinary person can hardly know, without consulting a dictionary, the semantic reasons for the different spellings of /s/ in *intercede* and *supersede* or in cases such as *session – cession, sensor – censor – censer, census – consensus, counsellor – councillor*.

BrE and AmE spelling differ here in a few words. BrE has *practise* (verb), *practice* (noun); AmE may have *practice* (verb). Both have *licence* or *license* (noun) and *license* (verb) and *justice, notice, service*, etc. BrE has *defence, offence*, AmE *defense, offense*; the adjectives are *defensive, offensive* for both.

6.6 Words with <dh> and <kh> have a distinctly exotic provenance: *dhobi, dhow, astrakhan, gymkhana, khaki, sheikh.*

Words with <gh> include one or two of Germanic origin such as *aghast, ghastly, ghost*, and some of more exotic origin: *dinghy* (surprisingly from Hindi), *gherkin, ghetto, ghoul, sorghum, spaghetti, yoghurt.*

Words with <ph> and <rh> have Greek elements: *morphology, philosophy, photography, xylophone*, etc. Initial <rh> occurs in: *rhapsody, rhetoric, rheumatism, rhinoceros, rhododendron, rhotic, rhythm*, and names from various sources: *Penrhyn, Rheims, Rhine, Rhondda.* Medial and final <rrh>, perhaps the most dreaded English spelling, is found in a number of medical terms, such as *catarrh, cirrhosis, diarrhoea/diarrhea, haemorrhage/hemorrhage.* The AmE spelling has reduced the <oe> and <ae> digraphs here to simple <e>.

For Irish and Scottish speakers and many AmE speakers, the <wh> spelling in *what, wheel*, etc. represents a voiceless fricative sound (pp. 7, 37). For them it contrasts with voiced /w/ in pairs such as *whether – weather, which – witch, whine – wine, whit – wit, whither – wither.* For speakers who do not make such a contrast <wh> is simply another spelling of /w/ and these pairs are homophones.

If we are to include foreign names, then there is also the <zh> ≡ /ʒ/ of *Brezhnev, Zhivago, Zhukov.*

UNIT 7
Some vowel spellings

7.1

1 <aer> ≡ /eə(r)/ – *aeration, aerial, aerobic, aeronaut, aerosol.* The <aer(o)-> spelling is a variant of <air> found in technical terms. Some are chiefly BrE rather than AmE, such as *aerodrome* and *aeroplane*; more familiar forms are *airfield, airplane.*

2 <augh> ≡ /ɔː/ – *caught, daughter, distraught, fraught, haughty, naughty, slaughter, taught.* The <gh> survives from the spelling of a lost consonant.

3 <ah> ≡ /ɑː/ – *bah, hurrah; Ahmed, Bahrain, Brahmin, Brahms, Mahler.* In many writing systems <h> is used to mark a long vowel. In English this use largely figures in exclamations and foreign names.

4 <al> ≡ /ɑː/ – before /m/ in *almond, alms, balmy, calm, embalmer, napalm, palm, psalm, qualms* and in *calf, half.* We can treat the <al> as a complex spelling unit.

5 <eau> ≡ /oʊ/ – is found in relatively recent French loanwords: *bureau, chateau, plateau, portmanteau, tableau, trousseau.*

6 <eigh> ≡ /eɪ/ – *eight, freight, neigh, neighbour, sleigh, weigh, weight.*

7 <ei> ≡ /iː/ – *ceiling, conceit, conceive, deceit, deceive, perceive, receipt, receive* and irregular *seize* (p. 54).

8 <eu> ≡ /(j)uː/ – *deuce, eucalyptus, feud, neutral, pneumonia, rheumatism, sleuth, therapeutic.*

9 <ey> ≡ /eɪ/ – *abeyance, conveyance, grey, heyday, prey, purveyor, surveying, they.*

10 <igh> ≡ /aɪ/ – *blight, bright, delight, fight, high, knight, light, might, night, right, sigh, thigh.* Irregular spellings often occur in very common words.

11 <oa> ≡ /oʊ/ – *approach, boast, cloak, coax, goat, groan, hoax, load, roast, shoal, soak, soap.*

12 <oir(e)> ≡ /wɑː(r)/ – *boudoir, escritoire, memoir, repertoire, reservoir, soiree.*

13 <oor> ≡ /ɔː(r)/ – *door, floor* and also *moor, poor,* for speakers who do not have /ʊə/.

14 <oo> ≡ /ʊ/ – *good, hood, stood, wood, boyhood, wool, foot, soot,* and (except for speakers in the north of England, who tend to have long /uː/ before /k/) *book, brook, cook, crook, forsook, hook, look, rookie, shook, took.*

15 <ough> ≡ /ɔː/ – *bought, brought, fought, nought, ought, sought, thought, wrought.*

16 <ough> ≡ /aʊ/ – *bough, plough* (BrE), *slough* ('bog'; in BrE), *sough. Plough* in AmE has a more regular spelling <plow>, but *bough* remains unchanged, so as not to add to the different meanings of <bow>. *Slough* has /uː/ in AmE, apart from New England.

17 <ough> ≡ /ʌf/ – *enough, rough, tough* and *slough* ('cast off').

18 <ough> ≡ BrE /ɒf/, AmE /ɑːf/ – *cough, trough.*

19 <ough> ≡ /uː/ – *through,* often spelt informally as <thro> or <thru>.

20 <ough> ≡ /oʊ/ – *although, dough, furlough, though.*

21 <oul> ≡ /ʊ/ – the three auxiliary verbs *could, should, would.*

22 <our> ≡ /aʊə(r)/ – *flour, hour, our, scour, sour.*

23 <our> ≡ /ʌr/ – *courage, flourish, nourish.*

24 <ui> ≡ /uː/ – *bruise, cruise, fruit, juice, recruit, sluice, suit.*

The complex spellings with <-gh->, such as <ough>, occur in a peculiar mix of very common words, such as *though, taught,* and archaic forms, such as *wrought, slough.*

7.2 The broad difference between the two samples is that words of two syllables with the ending <-ow> are native and those with final <-o> are non-native or slang. That would hardly help the ordinary speller, but the <-ow> words have a very distinct phonetic profile. They have no more than two syllables. They only have medial /d, n, nd, l, r/ preceded by a short stressed vowel: /d/ *widow*; /n/ *winnow*; /nd/ *window*; /l/ *follow*; /r/ *narrow.* These are all voiced consonants with the tongue-tip on the teeth-ridge (alveolar).

Any medial consonant that is *not* a tongue-tip consonant, alone or in a cluster, points to an <-o> spelling: *bingo, cargo, fresco, limbo,* etc. So does any voiceless consonant, such as /t/: *alto, ditto, presto, pronto*, etc. So does a previous long vowel, as in *beano, hero, judo, photo*, etc., or more than two syllables.

There are a couple of exceptions: *elbow* has <-ow> in spite of the /-lb-/ cluster and *bungalow* has three syllables. The abbreviated form *cello*, from *violoncello* keeps the <-o> of the original.

There are a dozen or so irregular words, mostly French in origin, outside the <-ow> and <-o> endings. For *bureau, chateau, plateau*, see p. 82. Also of French origin are some words with final empty consonant letters *apropos, depot, haricot*. Oddities are *cocoa, oboe, furlough*.

7.3   There is some uncertainty about the spelling of the plural of nouns ending in <-o>. We generally find:

- only <-os>: *concertos, quartos, radios, solos, sopranos*, etc.;
- only <-oes>: *dominoes, heroes, potatoes, tomatoes, torpedoes*, etc.;
- either <-os> or <-oes>: *cargo(e)s, commando(e)s, halo(e)s, tornado(e)s, volcano(e)s*, etc.

People are very willing to be dogmatic about this, but usage varies and there are few guidelines. The <-oes> form is not found in decidedly exotic words: *generalissimos, mulattos*; or in words where the plural is unusual: *indigos*; or in slang words: *boyos, buckos, dipsos, winos*. The only phonetic criterion is that if there is a vowel before the final /oʊ/, the <-oes> form does not occur: *radios, cameos*, certainly not *<cameoes>. The monosyllables *goes* and *noes* have the <e>-marked form. Insecure spellers frequently derive a singular spelling *<potatoe>, *<tomatoe> from the <-oes> plural form.

UNIT 8
Look-alikes and sound-alikes

8.2   The different pronunciations of these homographs are:

bow (/boʊ/ – /baʊ/)   buffet (/'bʊfeɪ/ –/'bʌfɪt/)
invalid (/ɪn'vælɪd/ – /'ɪnvəlɪd/)   lead (/liːd/ – /led/)
live (/lɪv/ – /laɪv/)   minute (/'mɪnɪt/ – /maɪ'njuːt/)
putting (/ʊ/ *put* – /ʌ/ *putt*)   read (/riːd/ – /red/)
row (/roʊ/ – /raʊ/)   tear (/teə(r)/ – /tɪə(r)/)
wind (/wɪnd/ – /waɪnd/)   wound (/wuːnd/ – /waʊnd/)

8.3   Quite different lexical words which have two-way identities as both homographs and homophones are homonyms:

bark /bɑːk/	(1 'b. of dog'; 2 'b. of tree')
barrow /'bæroʊ/	(1 'hill'; 2 'wheel-barrow')
bellows /'beloʊz/	(1 'fan'; 2 'shouts')
bound /baʊnd/	(1 'leap'; 2 'tied up')
cricket /'krɪkɪt/	(1 'game'; 2 'insect')
fell /fel/	(1 'cruel'; 2 'mountain'; 3 'tumbled')
fine /faɪn/	(1 'good'; 2 'penalty')
firm /fɜː(r)m/	(1 'solid'; 2 'company')

fit /fɪt/	(1 'healthy'; 2 'seizure')
flat /flæt/	(1 'level'; 2 'apartment')
hail /heɪl/	(1 'greet'; 2 'snow')
hamper /'hæmpə(r)/	(1 'impede'; 2 'basket')
last /lɑːst/	(1 'final'; 2 'cobbler's last')
leaves /liːvz/	(1 noun *leaf* ; 2 verb *leave*)
mews /mjuːz/	(1 from verb *mew*; 2 'back street')
mould /moʊld/	(1 'form'; 2 'mildew')
pants /pænts/	(1 'breaths'; 2 'trousers')
plane /pleɪn/	(1 'tree'; 2 'surface'; 3 'tool')
quail /kweɪl/	(1 'bird'; 2 'to cower')
quarry /'kwɒrɪ/	(1 'prey'; 2 'stone-quarry')
rest /rest/	(1 'repose'; 2 'remainder')
rose /roʊz/	(1 'flower'; 2 'nozzle'; 3 'got up')
row /roʊ/	(1 i.e. with oars; 2 'line')
stable /'steɪbl/	(1 i.e. for horses; 2 'constant'), etc.

Examples such as these clearly represent different lexemes. However, the full extent of the class of homonyms is bound to be indeterminate since it depends on what constitutes a difference of meaning.

8.4 Possible homophones are:

bruise, browse, choose, clause, copse, cruise, daze, flex, phlox, phrase, guise, nose, lax, lapse, lynx, please, praise, prise/prize, quartz, raise, size, tax, tease, treatise, wax

Some spellings show that the /s, z/ is not a suffix: word-final <-x> (*lax*, *lynx*) and what is sometimes called 'lexical <-e>' (*copse*, *please*). A <-y> before the /s, z/ shows it to be a suffix, since <y> is the alternative spelling to <i> at the end of a free-standing base form (*days*, *guys*).

8.5 Possible homophones are:

band, bald, build, bold, braid, brood, candid, chaste, coward, crude, duct, find, guest, mind, mist, mode, mustard, ode, paste, pact, side, staid, suede, tact, tide, toad, trust, wade, wield, word

Examples with final /aɪ/ before the /-d/ suffix, such as *tied – tide*, will not be homophones for those Scottish speakers who have two different variants, with [ae] in *tied* before the morpheme boundary and [ʌi] medially in *tide* (J. C. Wells, *Accents of English* (Cambridge: Cambridge University Press, 1982), p. 405). Scottish speakers will generally have a longer vowel showing the boundary in *brewed* [bruː+d] as distinct from *brood* [brud].

8.6 Possible homophones are:

border, boulder, dire, fissure, friar, grocer, hangar, hire, lever, meteor, rigo(u)r, savo(u)r, cellar, succo(u)r, tenor

8.7   Homophones in non-rhotic accents are:

arms, airier, ore, board, beater, carve, court, cork, cores, cord/cored, cheater, comber, cornier, curricular, farther, floor, formerly, fort, larva, lore, manner, nebular, pander, pore/pour, peninsular, roar, rotor, source, sore/soar, schemer, sort, spar, stork, torque, tuber, uvular

8.8   Most speakers will have homophones without the empty letters. Some are common enough, others rather archaic:

nave, need, new, night, not, no, wail, weal, weather, witch, wile, wine, wither, hole, rap, reek, reck, rest, retch, right, rite, ring, rote, rung, gage, gild, gilt, clime, jam, plum

8.9   Homophones are:

/iː/	beech, ceiling, creak, discreet, heal, meet, peace, sweet.
/ɪə/	bier, dear, here, pier, tear.
/eə/	bear, fare, flare, hair, pair/pear, stare, there.
/aɪ/	die, gyro, liar, cite/site, slight, stile, tyre.
/oʊ/	grown, load, loan, roe, rode, role, sow/so, soul, tow, yoke.
/ɔː/	oral, forth, horde, hoarse, coarse, warn, bawl, hall, maul, naught.
/aʊ/	bow, foul, flour.
/ɑː/	hart, barmy.
/uː/	plural, root, troupe, threw.
/juː/	due, hew, review.
/ɜː/	berth, fir, herd, purl, serf, tern, whorl, urn.

9.2

**UNIT 9
Sound-alike
affixes**

abundance, adherent, antecedent, benignant, blatant, brilliant, clairvoyant, component, confidence, consequence, consistency, covenant, dissonant, divergent, dominance, dormant, evidence, exorbitant, extravagant, exuberant, flamboyant, hesitant, immigrant, incessant, incident, indulgent, influence, insolvency, insurgent, itinerant, jubilant, lubricant, malignant, mutant, petulant, preponderant, recipient, recumbent, recurrent, redolent, redundancy, reference, relevance, residence, stimulant, transparent, valiant, vigilant

Stems ending in <-ul-> usually have <-ent>: *corpulent, flatulent, fraudulent, opulent, succulent, truculent*. Exceptions are *ambulance, petulant, stimulant*. Positive cues for <a> spellings are a stem-final /k, g, ʧ/ as in *significant, elegant, trenchant*, or any of the diphthongs /eɪ, aɪ, ɔɪ, aʊ/ as in *abeyance, reliance, annoyance, allowance*.

9.3   Free forms plus <-ible> after /d/, /t/, /s/ or /n/ include:

coercible	convertible	corrodible	corruptible	deducible
deductible	destructible	digestible	discernible	exhaustible
extendible	flexible	forcible	reversible	suggestible

9.4

adapter	agitator	alternator	astronomer	atomiser
barrister	chorister	commuter	condenser	congener
constrictor	curator	depositor	detector	elevator
geographer	improviser	inhibitor	insulator	liquefier
predecessor	rotator	spectator	subscriber	tutor

The agentive ending <-er> attaches to free forms, either native or Latinate: *commuter, drinker, killer, lover, liquefier, subscriber.* Occupational words made from Greek roots have <-er>: *astrologer, astronomer, biographer, geographer, philosopher*, where the <-er> replaces the <-y> of *astrology*, etc. *Beggar, liar* and *pedlar* are irregular; *peddler* is regular.

The ending <-or>, which only occurs in Latinate words, attaches to both free forms, as in *alternator, confessor, elevator, grantor, reactor, rotator*, and to bound forms (*predecessor, sponsor, tutor*). For some words dictionaries allow either spelling, with no semantic difference: *adviser – advisor, convener – convenor, vender – vendor.*

There are several distinct subgroups of Latinate <-or> words. The largest of these is of words ending in <-ator> formed from verbs ending in <-ate>: *creator, insulator, agitator*, etc. In some cases an equivalent verb is not found: *aviator, curator, spectator*, though it may be produced by back-formation as with *commentate* (from *commentator*). The <-er> suffix is only occasionally used after <-ate>: *collater, relater.*

The next largest group is words ending in <-ctor>, since several common roots happen to end in <ct>, (*detector, conductor, constrictor*). *Character* is not an agent.

A group of nouns ending in <-itor> are another well-defined subgroup (*inhibitor, capacitor, depositor*). The word *arbiter* is an exception: the /ə(r)/ is part of the base form (cf. *arbitration*).

9.5

auctioneer	bombardier	brigadier	buccaneer	cashier
engineer	gondolier	grenadier	mountaineer	mutineer
pamphleteer	profiteer	racketeer	sonneteer	volunteer

The <-eer> spelling is a productive stressed suffix that freely attaches to minimal free forms: *auctioneer, engineer, mountaineer, profiteer* and, absorbing the stem-final <-y>, *mutineer*. The ending <-eer> often has contemptuous overtones, such as *pamphleteer, sonneteer*, and always carries primary stress. The stressed suffix spelt <-ier>, as in *cashier, bombardier, grenadier, brigadier, gondolier*, unlike <-eer>, usually causes some reduction in the stem: /kə'ʃɪə(r)/, /brɪgə'dɪə(r)/, compared with /kæʃ/, /brɪ'geɪd/. It is not to be confused with the unstressed <-ier> of 'a pigeon *fancier*'.

9.6   Stressed <-VCCe> occurs in:

aquarelle	bagatelle	fontanelle	gazelle	cayenne
comedienne	cretonne	doyenne	bizarre	parterre
pelisse	crevasse	finesse	impasse	lacrosse

The ending <-enne> is feminine in *comedienne*, *doyenne*. People find it difficult to distinguish the masculine *doyen* from *doyenne* when anglicised, and it may simply depend on a stress difference: *LPD* /'dɔɪen/ and /dɔɪ'en/.

The stress shift to the first syllable in *kilogramme*, *programme* has probably encouraged a change of <-amme> to <-am>, which is the usual form in AmE spelling. In BrE the <-amme> spelling is losing ground. *Program* is certainly the form required in computer applications.

There are also some monosyllables with a final <-CCe> spelling: *gaffe*, *tulle*, *grippe*, *steppe*, *mousse*.

9.7

accomplice	acropolis	analysis	antithesis	apprentice
armistice	avarice	benefice	bodice	bronchitis
cannabis	chalice	coppice	cornice	cowardice
crevice	dentifrice	diagnosis	dialysis	edifice
emphasis	epidermis	genesis	hospice	jaundice
justice	lattice	liquorice	malice	metropolis
nemesis	novice	orifice	paralysis	parenthesis
poultice	practice	precipice	prejudice	synthesis

There is little guidance for the speller from word formation here. Only <-ice> is added to free forms, such as *cowardice*, *service*, and only <-ice> may change /s/ to /ʃ/ before suffixes: *auspicious*, *avaricious*, *beneficial*, *justiciary*, *malicious*, *novitiate*, *official*, *prejudicial*.

Words formed from recognisable Greek elements such as <dia->, <hypo-> will have <-is>. These may also have correspondences typical of Greek loans such as /f/ ≡ <ph>, /k/ ≡ <ch>, /θ/ ≡ <th> medially, and stressed /ɪ/ ≡ <y>. These meagre clues may prompt the correct spelling for *chrysalis*, *dialysis*, *hypothesis*. Given any such clue, you would not be tempted to spell *syphilis* as *<sifilice>.

9.9   There is a difference between *enquiry* as simply 'asking' and *inquiry* as a formal investigation: *enquiry office* 'asking about something' and *government inquiry* 'tribunal'. Cf. *He enquired after your health* and *They inquired into the price fixing*.

Similarly, *ensure* is the general meaning and *insure*, *insurance* is the restricted financial meaning: *The grant ensured her attendance* and *The grant insured her collection*.

10.1

Allan, Antony, Bryan, Carolyn, Katherine/Kathryn, Elizabeth, Geoffrey, Jon, Louis, Lynda, Marion, Margery

10.2 Many of these names are homophones with ordinary words, but irregular <C>-doubling and final <-e> are used to pad them out. They seem to gain advantage by having a certain written bulk. The name /leg/ rarely appears as *Leg*: the usual spelling is *Legge*.

<C>-doubling often occurs at the end of names with consonants /p, b, t, d, g, m, n, r/, which would otherwise have a single-letter spelling in final position. Final <-e> is often tacked on for good measure, as in *Bigge, Donne, Hobbes*. Final <-e> is also irregular in *Aske* after a two-consonant cluster or after a two-letter vowel spelling, as in *Crowe, Foyle*. This superfluous <-e> has archaic associations, which are sickeningly exploited in advertising: *<fayre>* (either for *fair* or *fare*), *<olde>*, *<shoppe>*.

The letter <y> is frequently used to spell /aɪ/ and /ɪ/, as in *Smyth, Symons, Wynne*. The <oy> spelling of /ɔɪ/ is normally final as in *coy, enjoy*, compared with *coin, enjoin*, but it often occurs medially in names such as *Boycott, Foyle*. So does <ay> in *Drayton, Hayter, Mayhew, Naylor, Paynter*.

10.4 If we look at the structure of the two lists of names, we can see interesting differences in sound and also in spelling. In the women's names there are five stop consonants and the average length of the names is 2.5 syllables. In the men's names there are thirteen stops and the average length in syllables is 1.6. The three names which do not have initial stress are women's: Diana, Elizabeth, Victoria. Of the ten women's names seven end in a vowel, but only one man's name does (if we exclude *Peter*).

If we look at the spelling instead of the sound, this difference is even more striking. All the men's names end in a consonant letter, but only one of the women's names does, *Elizabeth*, and that does not represent a stop.

These phonetic and graphic features conspire to produce an effect of 'softness' or 'less abruptness' in women's names and 'hardness' or 'more abruptness' in men's names. A personal name, written or spoken, is often more than just an arbitrary sign. It may reflect social attitudes to gender.

11.3 These are LEXICAL ERRORS involving confusion between similar sounding words. In (a) the string *<creator> is not simply a spelling error for *crater*. It is the right spelling of the wrong word. Simply to say that it contained the wrong correspondences /eɪ/ ≡ <ea> and /ə/ ≡ <or>, would be unhelpful. Similar confusions are (b) *<devoiced> for *divorced*, (c) *<liaisons> for *lesions*, (d) *<meteor> for *metier*, (e) *<reigns> for *reins*. This last example misunderstands a metaphor: not reigning as a king, but holding the reins of a horse.

In literature this kind of confusion may be used for comic effect as a MALAPROPISM (from French *mal à propos* 'inappropriate'). The term comes from the character Mrs. Malaprop in Sheridan's play *The Rivals* (1775). Examples from the play are: 'She's as headstrong as an *allegory on the banks of the Nile' (for *alligator*), 'He is the very *pineapple of perfection' (for *pinnacle*). As a comic device for making fun of the uneducated, this is as old as literature itself.

Malapropisms

11.4   These spelling errors are traceable to a particular pronunciation used by the speller. Spellers may forget that the spelling is based on a 'lento' (slow, formal) form of the word. Indeed, an 'allegro' (quick, colloquial) form may be the norm for their particular accent. Processes common in allegro forms are:

- consonant cluster simplification:

  *<bankrupcy>, *<pumkin>, *<strick>, *<reconise>, *<goverment>, *<distingtion>;

- smoothing of two adjacent vowels: *<pome>, *<vacume>;
- elision of /ə/: *<boundry>, *<litrature>;
- metathesis ('switching round'): *<anenome>, *<emnity>.

These are sometimes referred to as 'articulation errors'. This may, however, give the impression that an allegro pronunciation such as /ˈbaʊndrɪ/ is itself an 'error'. A better term would be INTERFERENCE ERRORS. This would also cover spelling errors due to the accent of the speaker.

Interference errors

A similar type of error is made by foreign learners, due to interference from the phonological system or from the writing system of their native language. Chinese-speakers have difficulty in pronouncing final consonant clusters, so they are likely to write 'the vowels *produce by ...', or '... can still be *perceive as ...', even when their knowledge of grammar should alert them to a further consonant /t/ or /d/, representing the suffix {-ed}.

11.5

(a) *<abberrant> (aberrant): the stem has an initial vowel <errant>, related to *err, error*. (p. 26).

(b) *<baronness> (baroness): confusion between <-ness>, as in <barren+ness> and the gender suffix <-ess> in <baron+ess>.

(c) *<begruge> (begrudge): <C>-doubling after a stressed short vowel (4.2, p. 74).

(d) *<chapple> (chapel): *chapel* is an early loan from Latin by way of French, which, unlike native words, has no <C>-doubling (pp. 22–3).

(e) *<comming> (coming): the verb *come* is irregular in having a short vowel with a long vowel spelling (cf. *dome*). In consequence it does not have <C>-doubling.

(f) *<deadden> (deaden): <C>-doubling does not normally occur when the preceding vowel is spelt with two letters (p. 18).

(g) *<gest> (guest): the <u> is needed as a marker to show that we have /gest/ and not /dʒest/ (p. 80).

(h) *<grammer> (grammar): <-er> is certainly the most common spelling of final /-ə(r)/, but derived forms with /æ/ such as *grammatical* should point to an <a> spelling (cf. p. 41).

(i) *<hateing> (hating): final <-e> as part of the long vowel spelling <a . . . e> is lost before a vowel-initial suffix such as <-ing> (p. 75).

(j) *<histery> (history): the endings in *ovary, mystery, history, injury* are homophones as /-ərɪ/ and so confusable. Derived forms that shift the stress, such as *ovarian, mysterious, historic, injurious*, will prompt the right vowel letter (cf. p. 41).

(k) *<induldge> (indulge): <C>-doubling does not occur after a consonant (p. 17).

(l) *<jumpt> (jumped): this is mistakenly a phonemic spelling. The past-tense morpheme in regular verbs is consistently written as <-ed>, even though it has three phonetic forms depending on the context: *jumped, begged, waited*, for example, have /-t/, /-d/ and /-ɪd/.

(m) *<maintainance> (maintenance): *maintain* does not preserve a constant spelling of a syllable with varying stress.

(n) *<medisine> (medicine): when /s/ varies with /k/, as in *medical*, the spelling is <c> (p. 81).

(o) *<prefered> (preferred): the final stressed <-er> of *confer, deter*, doubles the <r> before a vowel-initial suffix, as in *referral, deterrent, conferring*, unlike *differ, offer* (p. 79).

(p) *<ritch> (rich): *rich* is an early loan from French. The original final /ʃ/ has become /tʃ/, but without the <C>-doubling of native words such as *ditch, crutch*. Native *much, such* and *which* are also exceptional.

(q) *<sine> (sign): the <g> is an inert letter that is realised as /g/ in *signal, signature* (p. 80).

(r) *<wunder> (wonder): the first vowel took on an <o> spelling, unlike *blunder, thunder*, because the original <u> was difficult to separate from the three 'minim' vertical pen-strokes of <w> and the two of <n>.

12.1 On the normal printed page, the text would look like this:

As even Donald Duck can see, the main problem with a simple switch is that it's an all-or-none or on-or-off device. Why bother to understand its limitations?

UNIT 12
More than letters

12.2

(a) Reliable person wanted for light housekeeping job. Five days a week with weekends off.

(The unnecessary capital <P> may be an attempt to stress that both women and men could apply. The job is less likely in practice to be <lighthouse-keeping>. Both <days> and <weekends> are simple plurals. The compounds <housekeeping> and <weekend> are well established and need no hyphen.)

(b) The postman comes early on Tuesdays in summer, but the dustbin men can't always be relied on.

(The compounds <postman> and <dustbin> are well established, but not *<dustbinmen> (compare <highwaymen>). Capital letters are used for days of the week, but not usually for seasons, and <Tuesdays> here is a simple plural. Compare the possessive in <Tuesday's collection>. The apostrophe in <can't> points to missing letters. The normal verb form is <relied on> with no hyphen. It is not a complex modifier, as in <she was much relied-on>.)

(c) The Pennine Way at its best was altogether more demanding, so we were glad when journey's end was in sight.

(<Way> as a specific place requires a capital. There is no apostrophe in <its> as a possessive pronoun. The word <altogether> is a compound adverb. An apostrophe in <we're> would represent <we are>. The possessive of <journey's> requires an apostrophe. Written as one word, <insight> would be a compound noun.)

UNIT 13
American and British spelling

13.1 Mass nouns (not primarily 'countable'), such as *armour, behaviour, colour, favour, glamour, honour, humour, labour, odour, rigour, rumour, splendour, vapour, vigour*, traditionally spelt with <-our>, were given the ending <-or> in AmE spelling. It might be said in favour of the traditional BrE <-our> spelling that it usefully distinguishes these mass nouns from agent nouns ending in <-or>, such as *author, collector*. The case is complicated by various factors, however. Some mass nouns in medical use have <-or> in BrE spelling: *pallor, rigor, stupor*, as also do *languor, squalor, terror*. Conversely, some count nouns have <-our>: *harbour, parlour, tumour. Rigour* is spelt with <-our> in general BrE use and with <-or> as a medical term.

In some derived forms the <or> spelling is actually used in BrE: *armorial, coloration, laborious, vaporise*, but there are also *behavioural, colourful, flavoursome*.

13.2

artefact	carcase	gaol	judgement	manoeuvre
mould	moult	moustache	pyjamas	plough
smoulder	sulphur	tyre	waggon	woollen

14.2

aknolejmnt	butiqe	brodnng	conoser
exelsir	flumoxd	kiprs	neadd
languaj	orijn	fosfrus	sycolojy
rufaj	sfericl	holesm	riglng

UNIT 14
Spelling reform

14.4

aknolijment	buuteek	braudening	konesur
ekselseeor	flumoxt	kiperz	needid
langgwij	orrijin	fosforus	siekolojy
rufij	sferikal	hoelsum	rigling

FURTHER READING

All the topics included in this workbook, along with other aspects of English spelling, are covered in greater detail in:

> Edward Carney, *A Survey of English Spelling*, London: Routledge, 1994.

A study that takes a mainly American viewpoint is:

> D. W. Cummings, *American English Spelling: an Informal Description*, Baltimore: Johns Hopkins University Press, 1988.

For the historical development of traditional spelling over the centuries, see:

> D. G. Scragg, *A History of English Spelling*, Manchester: Manchester University Press, 1974

OED is a major reference work that is outstandingly useful for detailed information on English spelling and the origins and history of English words:

> J. A. H. Murray, H. Bradley, W. A. Craigie and C. T. Onions (eds), *The Oxford English Dictionary*, Oxford: Clarendon Press, 1933; 2nd edn 1989.

The twenty volumes are available with computer software on a CD-ROM disk.

The best dictionary of English pronunciation, quoted as *LPD*, is

> J. C. Wells, *Longman Pronouncing Dictionary*, London: Longman, 1990.

This gives a standard BrE (non-rhotic) and a standard AmE (rhotic) pronunciation. Ordinary dictionaries often give a respelling key of some kind to the pronunciation of words, but such apparatus is often more trouble to learn than standard phonetic symbols.

For looking up details of a particular English accent, a recommended source for those with some grounding in phonetics is the three-volume work:

> J. C. Wells, *Accents of English*, Cambridge: Cambridge University Press, 1982

Further reading on punctuation, including hyphens, apostrophes and capitals is:

> Eric Partridge, *You Have a Point There*, London: Hamish Hamilton, 1953

Further reading on the spelling reform proposals discussed in **Unit 14** is available from the Simplified Spelling Society (SSS):

> *Cut Spelling: a Handbook*, prepared by Christopher Upward and published by the SSS, 2nd edn, 1996
> *New Spelling 90* – Pamphlet 12 (1991) published by the SSS.

The text sample in New Spelling on p. xxx is from

> W. Ripman and W. Archer, *New Spelling: Being Proposals for Simplifying the Spelling of English Without the Introduction of New Letters*. (6th edn, revised by D. Jones and H. Orton), London: Pitman, 1948.

(The SSS address is 61 Valentine Road, Birmingham B14 7AJ, England.)

A detailed scheme for tidying up English spelling using the statistical regularities of the present system was developed by a Swedish scholar Axel Wijk in the 1960s and 1970s, but it received little backing. It was meant to serve the reader, rather than the writer.

> Axel Wijk, *Regularized English: an Investigation into the English Spelling Reform Problem*, Stockholm: Almqvist & Wiksell, 1959.
> —— *Regularized English: a Proposal for an Effective Solution of the Reading Problem in the English-speaking Countries*, Stockholm: Almqvist & Wiksell, 1977.

INDEX

UNIVERSITY COLLEGE WINCHESTER
LIBRARY